Pursuing a Plan B to Plan an "A" Future

STUDENT AND STUDENT-ATHLETE PLAN B BOOK

Inspiring Today's Future Leaders To An Understanding of Passion and Purpose Toward A Prosperous Career

ISBN 0-9837414-9-2

Copyright © 2018 Healthy Authors, Inc./Vitamin Foods, Inc. All rights reserved.

No part of this book may be reproduced or utilized in any form or by any means without permission in writing from the publisher, except for brief quotations used in a review.

DISCLAIMER PAGE

The information contained in this book is purposed to provide knowledge as a service to the public. It is not intended to guarantee that the resources and advice within this book will assure a person of securing a job position or career from reading the contents hereafter. The expressed viewpoints of the individuals depicted in this book are not claims that absolutely constitute what will occur in the lives of those who read their personal testimonies. Instead, this book is intended solely for general educational and informational purposes.

The health information herein is not intended to replace the medical advice of your physician. They are not intended to make, express, imply health or disease claims for this literary audience. You are advised to consult with your physician with regards to matters relating to your health, and in particular regarding matters that may require diagnosis or medical attention. DO NOT stop taking medications without first consulting with your physician. These statements have not been evaluated by the Food and Drug Administration.

See Our Other
FIGHT DISEASE WITH EASE BOOK TITLES ...

Specialized Healthy Recipe Books

1. **NOURISH YOURSELF TO HEALTH** – Eating Nourishing Foods to a Healthier You II

2. **NOURISH YOUR KIDS TO HEALTH** – Growing up a Child by Eating Nourishing Foods to a Healthy Adult

3. **FIGHTING DISEASE WITH EASE: 40 DAY MEAL PLAN** – Eating Yourself to a Healthier You

4. **ATHLETES**: Eat Your Way to a Competitive Advantage

5. **HIV/AIDS**: Fighting Disease with Ease - Eating Yourself to a Healthier You

6. **AGAVE SWEETENED HEALTHY RECIPES:** Fighting Disease with Ease – Eating Yourself to a Healthier You

7. **SICKLE CELL DISORDERS**: Fighting Disease with Ease – Eating Yourself to a Healthier You

www.vitaminfoodsinc.com

10 Disease & Condition Specific Healthy Recipe Books

8. CANCER: Fighting Disease with Ease – Eating Yourself to a Healthier You

9. CONSTIPATION & IRRITABLE BILE SYNDROME: Fighting Disease with Ease – Eating Yourself to a Healthier You

10. DIABETES: Fighting Disease with Ease – Eating Yourself to a Healthier You

11. DIGESTIVE PROBLEMS: Fighting Disease with Ease – Eating Yourself to a Healthier You

12. HEART DISEASE: Fighting Disease with Ease – Eating Yourself to a Healthier You

13. HIGH BLOOD PRESSURE: Fighting Disease with Ease – Eating Yourself to a Healthier You

14. HIGH CHOLESTEROL: Fighting Disease with Ease – Eating Yourself to a Healthier You

15. IMMUNE SYSTEM: Fighting Disease with Ease – Eating Yourself to a Healthier You

16. INFLAMMATION & ARTHRITIS: Fighting Disease with Ease – Eating Yourself to a Healthier You

17. INGREDIENT REFERENCE GUIDE TO COMBATING DISEASES AND CONDITIONS – Use these disease-fighting ingredients to create your own recipes

18. WEIGHT LOSS & OBESITY: Eating Yourself to a Healthier You

www.vitaminfoodsinc.com

SPECIAL THANKS

Make-A-Wish America Foundation, Jamie Sandys, Shaina Reeser, University of North Carolina at Charlotte, Kenya S., Koyah R., George F., Tamiko P., Katina T., Keith R., Archie B., National Basketball Association, Women's National Basketball Association, National Football League, Negro Baseball League, Major League Baseball, National Hockey League, Professional Auto Racing, Professional Bowling, Professional Cycling, Professional Golf, Professional Lacrosse, Professional Swimming, Professional Tennis, USA Track & Field, Professional Sports Leagues, Volleyball Leagues, National Collegiate Athletic Association Sports, High School Athletics, Little League Kid Sports Leagues, Pat Williams, Kara McIntosh, Milona A. Wall, Bartina L. Edwards, Mike Hill, Linda Probst, Ralph Burnett, Robert Craig Poole, Tim O'Riley, Dr. William Sears, Marvella Brown, Tunch Ilkin, Kelvin Torve, Josh Gibson, Sean L. Gibson, Ervin Rogers, Jr., Robert Jackson, Dr. Keith Henschen, Andrew Stockey, Joe Butler, William Tormay "Bill" Doorley.

PURPOSE OF THE PLAN B BOOK

The goal of this book is purposed to communicate to all students, especially, student-athletes that there is an abundance of occupations that need skilled specialists. Within this career exploration, there is a wide range of professional opportunities for students to analyze in the area of athletics. The exposure to these types of possibilities is the example students need to understand the existing occupational positions in operating sports activities and functions. These opportunities are available worldwide, and even, serviceable for our local communities' sporting needs.

So, whether you become a professional athlete or not, you can still have a career supporting the successful operation of sports industries. This can be achieved by working within job positions that can help to assist the functionality of sports processes.

Hopefully, this book will afford you the opportunity of becoming more informed of the bountiful choices available to you. A career in the sports world can assist in unlocking the passion, purpose, gifts, and skills that you possess. Therefore, a person's contribution to the sports world will make it more enjoyable for sports altogether.

INTRODUCTION

Greetings, I appreciate you taking the time to embark on this journey through reading this book to uncover some of the wonderful aspects of education, business, athletics, and life. During my youth, I aspired to be a student-athlete determined to reach the highest of heights on the basketball court, in addition to, striving to achieve the same type of success in the board rooms of business, I persistently sought to grasp both of these goals. Many of you that are in school have the same thoughts I had growing up. The innermost desires of your childhood, adolescence, and young adulthood can be the fuel to your passion and the drive necessary to propel you toward making your fantasies your realities.

Statistics are vital to understanding the conditions that many of the nation's student-athletes are facing: Did you know that over 99% of high school student-athletes will not make it to the professional level in their sport? Well, the stark reality is that 99.4% of the 7.8 million current high school student-athletes will not make it to the pros: only 0.6% of high school student-athletes will make it to the pros, and fewer than 2% of collegiate athletes will make it to the pros. Therefore, it is essential that student-athletes are made aware of the abundant number of career opportunities which are present in the workplace for them, especially, in the professional world of sports outside of the "playing field". However, the aforementioned statistics don't even account for injuries that may threaten the continuance of a playing career within an athlete's experience. So, even if a student-athlete does not reach the professional level as an athlete, he or she can still pursue a career in the world of sports. Professional career opportunities in education, business, sports-related jobs "off the field or outside of the court", and finding work in the arts is a reality available for our future workforce.

Therefore, it brings me great joy that you have opened this book to read of the experiences of successful professionals in education, business, sports, and the arts. They speak to the essentials of life, and what it takes to obtain career success for the purpose of fulfilling and sustaining their lives. My hope is predicated upon introducing and/or reinforcing to you of the bountiful career choices in the world of sports. Whether you're seeking to become a professional athlete, a sports enthusiast who wants to be a sports professional "off the field", or even if you are a person who doesn't enjoy sports at all, it's important for you to know that there are job opportunities which can lead you to satisfy the career of your dreams in sports for anyone.

Students and student-athletes, you, are our next generation, and informing, educating and equipping you with knowledge, understanding, experiential insight and resources are what is vital to assist you in acquiring the lofty personal ideals that you all envision on or off the field or in or out of the classroom. This book is designed to provide elements of the aforementioned to motivate and inspire students and student-athletes to your full potential toward your career passions and career aspirations.

The focus of this book is purposed to provide you with specific career options as a Plan B. So, you can survey, study, self-assess and apply your interest toward a career path presented in this **Plan B Book** while you're pursuing your loftiest goals in sports. In the event your athletic aspirations do not manifest into your reality, you have a career path that has already been presented to you, investigated and researched by your exploration through this book for your specific Plan B. This will enable you to make a smoother transition into the field of your choice, therefore producing a Plan "A" future.

Our nation's future will, soon, be in the hands of our country's most cherished assets, you, our current students. My hope centers on believing that as you continue to read this book that you will be enriched and encouraged. So, develop a plan to acquire the "field of dreams" not only on the court but, also, in the field of business or whatever career path that you choose for yourself to obtain a prosperous future!!

----All the best, A message from the author: David Burnett

TABLE OF CONTENTS

PURPOSE OF THIS BOOK..................................6

INTRODUCTION PAGE 7-8

TABLE OF CONTENTS..............................9-10

SPORTS-RELATED JOBS WITH THE
STRONGEST GROWTH..................................11

21 OF THE FASTEST GROWING
SPORTS JOBS..................................12-14

THE TOP 10 SPORTS CAREERS FOR NON-
ATHLETES..................................15

TOP 10 CITIES WITH THE HIGHEST
SPORTS-RELATED JOB GROWTH..................16

TOP 10 COLLEGES FOR
SPORTS LOVERS..................................17

CATEGORIES OF JOB POSITIONS
IN ATHLETICS 18

ACCOUNTING..................................19-24

BUSINESS..................................25-39

COLLEGE POSITIONS..................................40-46

FITNESS..................................47-57

GRADUATE ASSISTANT POSITIONS..................58-69

HEALTH & WELLNESS AND NUTRITION..................70-82

INTERNSHIPS..................83-92

PRO SPORTS SPECIFIC POSITIONS..................93-111

SOCIAL MEDIA..................112-124

SPORTS EQUIPMENT..................125-145

SPORTS MANAGEMENT..................146-153

SPORTS MEDIA..................154-168

SPORTS TELEVISION..................169-181

GLOSSARY..................182-186

REFERENCE PAGE..................187

VISIT OUR WEBSITE..................188

INDEX..................189-193

FACTS ABOUT JOBS IN SPORTS

The Sports-Related Jobs With The Strongest Growth
According to Kathryn Dill

Jobs across all sports-related industries are up 12.6% since 2010--more than double the growth in the national job market, according to a report released by CareerBuilder and Economic Modeling Specialists. **Average earnings across these sports occupations are --$78,455**—which also top the national average of $57,947.

Additionally, sports jobs have a strong "multiplier effect," creating job growth in other fields beyond athletics. The report states that 100 new sports-related jobs in Pittsburgh have the ability to create $46.2 million in earnings for the city, as well as 422 jobs in "construction, health care, sales, food preparation, and maintenance."

22 of the Fastest Growing Sports Jobs

According to Debra Auerbach

Occupational breakdown

Six industries, 21 sports-related positions exist that are essential to your game day experience, including:

1. Meeting, convention, and event planners
Employed in sports-related industries (2010): 3,685
Employed in sports-related industries (2014): 5,136
Change (2010-2014): 39 percent

2. Concierges
Employed in sports-related industries (2010): 1,071
Employed in sports-related industries (2014): 1,462
Change (2010-2014): 37 percent

3. Audio and video equipment technicians
Employed in sports-related industries (2010): 6,491
Employed in sports-related industries (2014): 8,268
Change (2010-2014): 27 percent

4. Market research analysts and marketing specialists
Employed in sports-related industries (2010): 1,818
Employed in sports-related industries (2014): 2,308
Change (2010-2014): 27 percent

5. Laborers and freight, stock and material movers, hand
Employed in sports-related industries (2010): 6,491
Employed in sports-related industries (2014): 8,212
Change (2010-2014): 27 percent

6. Public address system and other announcers
Employed in sports-related industries (2010): 2,040
Employed in sports-related industries (2014): 2,530
Change (2010-2014): 24 percent

7. **Secretaries and administrative assistants, except legal, medical and executive**
Employed in sports-related industries (2010): 5,193
Employed in sports-related industries (2014): 6,417
Change (2010-2014): 24 percent

8. **Agents and business managers of artists, performers, and athletes**
Employed in sports-related industries (2010): 9,493
Employed in sports-related industries (2014): 11,641
Change (2010-2014): 23 percent

9. **Radio and television announcers**
Employed in sports-related industries (2010): 1,174
Employed in sports-related industries (2014): 1,428
Change (2010-2014): 22 percent

10. **Producers and directors**
Employed in sports-related industries (2010): 2,881
Employed in sports-related industries (2014): 3,490
Change (2010-2014): 21 percent

11. **Ushers, lobby attendants, and ticket takers**
Employed in sports-related industries (2010): 25,441
Employed in sports-related industries (2014): 30,388
Change (2010-2014): 19 percent

12. **Accountants and auditors**
Employed in sports-related industries (2010): 1,952
Employed in sports-related industries (2014): 2,314
Change (2010-2014): 19 percent

13. **Janitors and cleaners, except maids and housekeeping cleaners**
Employed in sports-related industries (2010): 7,299
Employed in sports-related industries (2014): 8,574
Change (2010-2014): 17 percent

14. **Public relations specialists**
Employed in sports-related industries (2010): 3,301
Employed in sports-related industries (2014): 3,875
Change (2010-2014): 17 percent

15. **Maintenance and repair workers, general**
Employed in sports-related industries (2010): 3,565
Employed in sports-related industries (2014): 4,160
Change (2010-2014): 17 percent

16. **Security guards**
Employed in sports-related industries (2010): 13,975
Employed in sports-related industries (2014): 16,253
Change (2010-2014): 16 percent

17. **Office clerks, general**
Employed in sports-related industries (2010): 6,068
Employed in sports-related industries (2014): 7,054
Change (2010-2014): 16 percent

18. **General and operations managers**
Employed in sports-related industries (2010): 5,611
Employed in sports-related industries (2014): 6,476
Change (2010-2014): 15 percent

19. **Amusement and recreation attendants**
Employed in sports-related industries (2010): 5,336
Employed in sports-related industries (2014): 6,110
Change (2010-2014): 15 percent

20. **Coaches and scouts**
Employed in sports-related industries (2010): 7,769
Employed in sports-related industries (2014): 8,349
Change (2010-2014): 7 percent

21. **Athletes and sports competitors**
Employed in sports-related industries (2010): 9,535
Employed in sports-related industries (2014): 9,775
Change (2010-2014): 3 percent

The Top 10 Sports Careers for Non-Athletes
According Bestschools.org

1. Athletic Trainer - *Median annual salary:* $45,630 per year
2. Coach - *Median annual salary*: $31,460 (BLS—*Note:* This figure includes coaches in all sports at all institutions; successful coaches in the major sports, such as football & basketball, at big-name schools, may earn much higher salaries, up to seven figures.)
3. Fitness Director - *Median annual salary:* $38,160
4. Photojournalist/Sports Photographer - *Median annual salary:* $34,070
5. Physical Therapist - *Median annual salary:* $85,400
6. Recreation Worker - *Median annual salary*: $23,870
7. Sporting Event Planner/Coordinator - *Median annual salary:* $47,350
8. Sports Psychologist - *Median annual salary:* $75,230
9. Statistician - *Median annual salary*: $80,500
10. Umpire/Referee - *Median annual salary:* $25,660

Top 10 Cities with the Highest Sports-Related Job Growth
According to Fobres.com

1. Pittsburgh, PA
2. Jacksonville, FL
3. Atlanta, GA
4. Buffalo, NY
5. Boston, MA
6. Cincinnati, OH
7. Denver, CO
8. Miami, FL
9. Dallas, TX
10. Philadelphia, PA

Top 10 Colleges for Sports Lovers
According to Money Magazine and Sports Illustrated

1. Stanford University
2. University of Notre Dame
3. University of Michigan
4. Duke University
5. University of Virginia
6. University of North Carolina – Chapel Hill
7. University of Florida
8. Middlebury University
9. Yale University
10. Bowdoin College

JOBS & INTERNSHIPS IN SPORTS

CATEGORIES OF JOB POSITIONS IN ATHLETICS

Contact your local youth sports organizations, schools, universities, professional sports teams, social organizations, sports stores, engineering occupations, construction companies, financial planning institutions, and health & wellness corporations and food and beverage companies for employment or internship opportunities in the world of sports.

Did you know that over 99.4% of the 7.8 million high school student-athletes will not make it to the professional level in their sport? Additionally, only 2% of collegiate athletes will become professional athletes. In addition to these student-athlete statistics, multiple studies report that up to 75% of students entering college change their major before graduation, and 50% will change their major more than two times during a three year period. So, let's journey together unto a pathway leading to an opportunity of **over 3,000 career job positions** within this book for our promising future leaders to explore.

ACCOUNTING JOBS

Accounting Analyst ~ Accounting Compliance ~ Administrator ~ Accounting Associate ~ Accounting Clerk ~ Accounting Coordinator ~ Accounting Trainee ~ Account Executive – Consumer Sales ~ Account Executive – Corporate Sales ~ Account Executive – Group Sales ~ Account Executive-Ticket Sales ~ Account Manager ~ Account Marketing Manager ~ Accounts Receivable Processor ~ Accounts Receivable Manager ~ Accounts Receivable Supervisor ~ Administrator – Employee Accountants ~ Bookkeeper ~ Cash Room Attendant ~ Construction Project Accountant ~ Director of Accounting ~ Human Resources Analyst ~ Junior Accountant ~ Junior Staff Accountant ~ Payroll Analyst ~ Revenue Accountant ~ Seasonal Accountant ~ Senior Accountant ~ Senior Cost Accountant ~ Staff Accountant ~ Treasury & Payroll Accountant.

SPORTS PROFESSIONAL PROFILE
ALL STUDENTS, AND PARTICULARLY, STUDENT-ATHLETES, "DO YOU HAVE A PLAN B?"

Professional Occupation Questionnaire for Student Academic & Career Developmental Exposure

Name: PAT WILLIAMS

Your Current Job Title and/or the Job You're Most Known for Participating: CO-FOUNDER AND SENIOR VICE PRESIDENT OF THE NBA'S ORLANDO MAGIC
Number of Years in Current Position or Number of Years in the Position You're Most Known for Participating: 32 YEARS
List the Previous Job Titles You've Had: GENERAL MANAGER, CHICAGO BULLS; GENERAL MANAGER, ATLANTA HAWKS; GENERAL MANAGER, PHILADELPHIA 76ERS
List College Major(s), Master Degree(s), Doctoral Degree(s): Bachelor of Science (BS), WAKE FOREST (1962); MS INDIANA UNIVERSITY (1964)

1. **Who inspired you the most?** My parents inspired me the most.

2. **What motivated you during the pursuit of your career?** I always wanted to be considered a winner, and I wanted to reach the highest level possible in my sports pursuits.

3. **Who or what influenced you to achieve your goal(s) as a professional?** Bill Veeck influenced me to achieve my goals.

4. **What goal(s) did you set for yourself in attempting to reach your career aspiration(s)?** I stay in good shape physically, read good books and surround myself with the sharpest people.

5. **What were your greatest strengths that you executed as a professional within your career?** My greatest strengths that I execute are energy and enthusiasm.

6. **What most challenged you during your journey to becoming the professional in your occupation?** To produce a winning team is what challenged me most.

7. **How did you manage your weaknesses with your occupation?** I surrounded myself with the best people I could that had skills that I lacked.

8. **How important was time management in performing well on your job?** Time management was critically important.

9. **How much of your educational background factored into obtaining success in your field of work?** Without my two educational stops, I never could have accomplished my goals.

10. **What was your greatest accomplishment as a professional?** My greatest accomplishment was winning the 1983 NBA title.

11. **Why did you or do you work?** I love what I'm doing.

12. What did you or do you value most about your occupation? I valued the relationships that I have built throughout my career the most.

13. What projects are you working on now? I continue to write books, including an upcoming book entitled *Character Carved in Stone*.

14. Feel free to add any additional comments: Figure out what your greatest talent is and determine where your greatest passion lies; find where those two intersect and you will have a fulfilling life.

STUDENT AND STUDENT-ATHLETE PLAN B BOOK
ALL STUDENTS, AND PARTICULARLY, STUDENT-ATHLETES, "DO YOU HAVE A PLAN B?

Professional Occupation Questionnaire for Student Academic & Career Developmental Exposure

Name: Kara McIntosh

Your Current Job Title and/or the Job You're Most Known for Participating: Human Resources & Payroll Associate

Number of Years in Current Position or Number of Years in the Position You're Most Known for Participating: 5 years

List College Major(s), Master Degree(s), Doctoral Degree(s): Bachelor of Science in Business Management

1. **Who inspired you the most?** My parents inspired me most, as they both had a tremendous work ethic.

2. **What motivated you during the pursuit of your career?** I desired independence, and that motivated me.

3. **Who or what influenced you to achieve your goal(s) as a professional?**

    My parents were most influential to me in achieving my goals.

4. **What goal(s) did you set for yourself in attempting to reach your career aspiration(s)?**
    Attending college and obtaining a degree were the goals I set for myself.

5. **What were your greatest strengths that you executed as a professional within your career?**
The ability to work well with others was one of my greatest strengths.

6. **What most challenged you during your journey to becoming the professional in your occupation?**
Finding an industry that felt like a good fit for me, is what challenged me most during my journey.

7. **How did you manage your weaknesses within your occupation?**
I managed my weakness through self-evaluation and collaboration with colleagues.

8. **How important was time management in performing well on your job?** Time management is essential to my profession, as the nature of my role is fast paced.

9. **How much of your educational background factored into obtaining success in your field of work?** My educational background was very relevant as I studied human resources and finance.

10. **What was your greatest accomplishment as a professional?** My greatest accomplishment was graduating from school and finding success in a career path that I enjoyed.

11. **Why did you or do you work?** The reason I work is to support myself while obtaining self-fulfillment.

12. **What did you or do you value most about your occupation?** I get to help others.

BUSINESS JOBS

50/50 Sales Representative ~ Account Receivables Administrator ~ Account Service Executive – Audio ~ Administrative Assistant ~ Ad Operations Coordinator ~ Ad Operations Manager ~ Affiliate Marketing Director ~ Ambassador Assistantship ~ Analyst-Financial Operations ~ Aquatics & Program Director ~ Aquatics Director ~ Associate Annual Campaign Director ~ Associate Athletic Director ~ Associate Athletic Director for Annual Giving ~ Associate Athletic Director of Compliance ~ Associate Director of Athletics ~ Associate of Athletics Marketing ~ Associate Director Video Production ~ Associate Digital Producer ~ Associate Photo Editor ~ Associate Producer ~ Associate Public Relations Manager ~ Association Aquatics Director ~ Assistant Athletic Director ~ Assistant Athletic Trainer ~ Assistant Athletics Director Broadcasting & Production ~ Assistant Colorist ~ Assistant Director of Athletic Communications ~ Assistant Director of Communications ~ Assistant Director of Marketing ~ Assistant Director of Strategic Communications ~ Assistant Director of Development ~ Assistant Director of Ticket Operations ~ Assistant General Manager ~ Assistant Integration Producer 1 ~ Assistant Managing Editor ~ Assistant Product Developer ~ Assistant Sales Manager ~ Assistant to the Athletic Trainer ~ Athletic Club Assistant Director ~ Athletic Compliance Coordinator ~ Athletic Department Program Coordinator ~ Athletic Director ~ Athletic Fields Assistant ~ Athletic Fund Coordinator ~ Athletic Fund Director ~ Athletic Trainer ~ Athletics Business Services Manager ~ Athletics Communications Director ~ Athletics Communications Assistant ~ Athletics Development Associate ~ Athletics Development Coordinator ~ Athletics Development Leadership Gift Officer ~ Athletics Director, Athletics Producer - Creative Video ~ Athletics Ticket Services Assistant ~ Attorney ~ Authentics Sales Lead ~ Author ~ Ballpark Operations Event Staff ~ Banking Analyst ~

Bootcamp Marketing Director ~ Box Office Manager ~ Branch Executive Director ~ Brand Ambassador ~ Brand Marketing Manager ~ Broadcast Operations Senior Manager ~ Budgeting Planning Coordinator ~ Business Analyst ~ Business Development Associate ~ Business Development Coordinator ~ Business/Financial Analyst ~ Business Intelligence Analyst ~ Business Intelligence Manager ~ Business Office Assistant ~ Business Office Assistant Director ~ Business Office Assistantship ~ Business Operations Coordinator ~ Business Systems Analyst ~ Camp & Sports Manager ~ Category Marketing Specialist ~ Chairman of the Board of Directors – Youth Organization ~ Chief Development Officer ~ Client Operations Executive ~ Client Strategy Associate Manager ~ Client Strategy Senior Manager ~ Club Digital Strategy Coordinator ~ Club Manager (Sports) ~ Club Operations Coordinator ~ City League Director ~ Club Repair Associate ~ College Area Scout ~ Communications Assistant ~ Communications Director ~ Communications Summer Assistant ~ Community Outreach Coordinator ~ Compensation Analyst ~ Compliance Assistant Director ~ Consumer & Business Engagement Vice-President ~ Content Assistant Director ~ Content Associate ~ Content Coordinator ~ Content – Vice President ~ Contract Administrator ~ Controller – Sports Management ~ Coordinator of Athletic Multimedia ~ Coordinator for Student-Athlete Success ~ Coordinating Road Producer ~ Copywriter – Digital Acquisition ~ Corporate Partnership Coordinator ~ Corporate Sales – Account Executive ~ Corporate Sales & Service Director ~ Corporate Sales Territory Manager ~ Corporate Sponsorship Sales Property Assistant ~ Creative Media Coordinator ~ Creative Director (Media) ~ Customer Experience Representative ~ Customer Service Representative ~ Data Analytics Manager ~ Database Administrator ~ Database Infrastructure Director ~ Deputy Athletics Director ~ Development Assistant ~ Development Coordinator ~ Development Officer ~ DevOps Manager ~ Digital Associate Producer ~ Digital Archive Coordinator ~ Digital Communications Manager ~ Digital Content

Coordinator ~ Digital Content Director ~ Digital Content Editor ~ Digital Content Producer ~ Digital Editor in Chief ~ Digital Media & Art Producer ~ Digital Media Coordinator ~ Digital Media Executive Assistant ~ Digital Sports Director ~ Digital Video Coordinator ~ Digital Marketing Analyst ~ Digital Marketing Associate ~ Digital Marketing Associate Manager ~ Digital Marketing Director ~ Digital Marketing Freelancer ~ Digital Marketing Innovation Manager ~ Digital Marketing Manager ~ Digital Marketing Project Manager ~ Digital Marketing Senior Manager ~ Digital Marketing Strategist ~ Digital Media Coordinator ~ Digital Media Producer ~ Digital Media Producer/Editor ~ Digital Retail Planning Director ~ Digital Sales Analytics Manager ~ Digital Sales Director ~ Director of Accounts – Sports Teams ~ Director of Annual Giving (Athletic Fund) ~ Director of Athletic Advancement ~ Director of Athletic Development ~ Director of Athletic Communications ~ Director of Athletic Operations ~ Director of Athletics ~ Director of Content Production ~ Director of Digital Media Services ~ Director of Business Operations ~ Director of Business Analytics – Ticket Operations ~ Director of Business Planning ~ Director of Communications ~ Director of Community Relations ~ Director of Development ~ Director of Digital Media Services ~ Director of Entertainment & Sports Relations ~ Director of Executive Recruiting ~ Director Finance ~ Director-Financial Planning & Analyst ~ Director of Graphic Design ~ Director of Marketing ~ Director of Marketing & Strategy ~ Director of People & Culture ~ Director of Premium Marketing Ecommerce (Web) Analyst ~ Director of Strategy ~ Director of Video Production ~ Diversity & Inclusion Associate Director Athletics ~ eCommerce Technology Manager ~ Direct-To-Consumer Strategy & Business Ops ~ Director to Consumer Business Operations & Analytics ~ Ecommerce Junior Marketing Manager ~ Editor ~ Email Marketing Manager ~ Email Marketing Specialist ~ Employee Relations Associate ~ Engineering Director ~ Engineering Project Coordinator ~ Engineering Services Coordinator ~ Enterprise Account Executive ~ Entry-Level Business Data Analyst ~

Equipment Design Director ~ Executive Director ~ Executive Director Communication Foundation & Vice President of Communications ~ Executive Producer Digital Marketing ~ Experience Design Manager ~ Events Coordinator ~ Events & Facilities Assistant ~ Events & Facilities Security ~ Events Development Director ~ Event Production Director ~ Event Sales Administration ~ Event Sales Coordinator ~ Event Sales Manager ~ Event Time Ticket Sales Staff ~ Facilities and Events Assistant ~ Fantasy Sports Operations Manager ~ Field Marketing Manager ~ Field Sales Representative ~ Financial Analyst ~ Financial Operations Administrator ~ Financial Reporting Coordinator ~ Finance Coordinator ~ Finance Office Assistant ~ Finance Systems Administrator ~ Fitness Specialist ~ Fixed Asset Accountant ~ Food and Nutrition Editor ~ Footwear Lead ~ Franchise Business Coach ~ Freelance Production Assistant ~ Front Desk Sales ~ Fundraising Coordinator ~ Game and Event Setup Crew ~ Game Designer ~ Game Director ~ Game Night Operations Manager ~ Game Night Public Relations Staff ~ Game Night Staff ~ Game Operations Coordinator ~ General Manager ~ General Manager/Fitness Manager ~ General Manager of Sports Franchises ~ General Manager of Ticket Sales ~ Global Benefits Operations Analyst ~ Global Digital Marketing Manager ~ Global Logistics Analyst ~ Global Logistics Manager ~ Global Marketing Manager ~ Global Public Relations Manager ~ Global Software Asset Manager ~ Global Store Development Lead ~ Global Strategy – Vice President ~ Global Trade & Logistics Specialist ~ Golf Shop Assistant ~ Graphic Design Coordinator ~ Graphic Design Lead ~ Graphic Design Assistant ~ Graphics Production Assistant ~ Group Event Coordinator ~ Group Sales Coordinator ~ Growth Management Director ~ Growth Marketing Director ~ Guest Services Event Staff ~ Head Athletic Trainer ~ Head Athletic Trainer (Football) ~ Head of Global Marketing ~ Head of Property Sales ~ Head of Sales Operations ~ Head of Sponsorship Sales ~ Health Fitness Program Manager ~ Health Fitness Specialist ~ Healthy Athletes Program Manager ~ Hospitality Manager ~ Hotel

Market Manager ~ Human Resources Administrator ~ Human Resources Coordinator ~ Human Resources Generalist ~ Human Resources Manager ~ Human Resources Operations Coordinator ~ Human Resources Vice-President ~ In-Game Entertainment Manager ~ In-Game Host ~ Inside Sales Associate ~ Inside Sales Consultant ~ Inside Sales Manager ~ Inside Sales Representative ~ Inside Sales Ticket Representative ~ Insights & Strategy Planner ~ Instrumentation Product Manager ~ Intercollegiate Athletics Assistant Associate Director ~ Intercollegiate Athletics Associate Director ~ Intermediate Accountant ~ Internal Audit Manager ~ Internal Communications Director ~ International Digital Marketing Manager ~ International Teams Coordinator ~ Inventory Lead Product Manager ~ Inventory – Sales Auditor ~ Investment Operations Coordinator ~ IT Administrator ~ IT Financial Analyst ~ Junior Marketing Manager ~ Junior Staff Accountant ~ Lead Instructor ~ League Coordinator ~ League Monitors ~ League Operations Coordinator ~ Learning Development Manager ~ Learning & Development Manager ~ Live Events Associate Producer ~ Live Events Producer ~ Live Operations Director ~ Logistics Account Manager ~ Logistics – Claims Analyst ~ Logistics Planner ~ Logistics Specialist ~ Manager-Event Finance ~ Manager of Athletic Media Relations ~ Manager of Corporate Communications ~ Manager of Event Sales ~ Manager of Procurement Operations ~ Manager of Sports Officials ~ Managing Editor ~ Manufacturing Product Manager ~ Marketing & Communications Business Coordinator ~ Marketing and Sales Director ~ Marketing Lead – Sports Management ~ Marketing Manager ~ Marketing Junior Manager ~ Marketing Partnerships Digital Strategist ~ Marketing Programs Specialist ~ Marketing Specialist ~ Marketing Support Specialist ~ Marketing Technology & Reporting Senior Analyst ~ Marketing Vice President ~ Master Control Operator ~ Media Operations Manager ~ Media Relations Director ~ Media Sales Representative ~ Member Services Associate ~ Member Services Specialist ~ Member Services Supervisor ~

Membership Advisor ~ Membership Director ~ Membership and Marketing Director ~ Membership Sales Advisor ~ Merchandise Coordinator ~ Mobile Game Designer ~ Mountain Hardwear Head of Sales ~ Multi-Platform Producer ~ Multi-Platform Production Assistant ~ National Sales Manager ~ National Sales – Vice President ~ New Business Representative ~ News Editor ~ News & Sports Office Administrator ~ New Product Development Associate ~ NHL Social Media Community Manager ~ Part Time Distribution Specialist ~ Product Logistics Coordinator ~ Product Logistics Manager ~ Product System Operations Lead ~ Program Manager ~ Office Assistant ~ Office Manager ~ On-Call Producer ~ Operations Coordinator ~ Operations Leader ~ Operations Specialist ~ Partner Fulfillment Game Operations ~ Outdoor Apparel Senior Design Manager ~ Partnership Account Manager ~ Partnership Sales & Service Executive ~ Partnership Strategy Coordinator ~ Part-Time Production Assistant I ~ Photo Studio Operations Coordinator ~ Pilates Instructor ~ Platform Optimization Coordinator ~ Platinum Sales Manager ~ Post Production Coordinator ~ Premium-Finance Manager ~ Principal Management Consultant ~ Process & Technology Director ~ Product Manager ~ Production Art Coordinator ~ Production Coordinator ~ Production Assistant ~ Production Associate ~ Production Support Representative ~ Program Marketer ~ Project Manager ~ Project Multimedia Editor ~ Project Photo Digital Editor ~ Pro Sports Fantasy Researcher ~ Public Affairs Executive Assistant ~ Public Relations Director ~ Purchasing Manager ~ Real Estate Development Director ~ Real Estate Financial Analyst ~ Regional Health Fitness Spec ~ Regional Vice-President – Operations for Stadium/Arenas & Convention Centers ~ Research Analyst ~ Research Designer ~ Resident Camp Program Director ~ Retail Accountant ~ Retail Brand Manager ~ Retail Coordinator ~ Retail Digital Marketing Lead ~ Retail Divisional – Vice President ~ Retail Game Day Associate (Part-Time) ~ Retail Sales Associate ~ Retail Sales Associate Lead ~ Retail Sales Specialist ~ Retail Store Operations Director ~ Retail Website

Associate ~ Risk Analyst ~ Run Club Coordinator ~ Runner Services- Assistant Manager ~ Sales Academy Executive ~ Sales Account Executive ~ Sales/Account Manager ~ Sales and Service Consultant ~ Sales Associate ~ Sales Development Specialist ~ Sales Enablement & Operations Lead ~ Salesforce Administrator ~ Sales Lead ~ Sales/Marketing Associate ~ Sales Operations Associate ~ Sales Operations Coordinator ~ Sales Operations Manager ~ Sales Manager ~ Sales Representative ~ Sales Specialist ~ Sales Team Lead ~ Scheduling Operations Coordinator ~ Seasonal Operations Coordinator ~ Seasonal Sales Associate ~ Seasonal Sales/Group Sales Assistant ~ Senior Accountant ~ Senior Aquatics Director ~ Senior Associate Athletic Director ~ Senior Audit Analyst ~ Senior Business Data Analyst ~ Senior Cost Accountant ~ Senior Director (Media) ~ Senior Director Sports Marketing ~ Senior Remote Operations Producer ~ Senior Human Resources Business Partner ~ Senior Media Relations Associate ~ Senior Operations Research Analyst ~ Senior Producer/Editor ~ Senior Property Accountant ~ Senior Retail Brand Experience Manager ~ Senior Tax Analyst ~ Senior Technical Project Manager ~ Senior Video Editor ~ Senior Video Graphics Designer ~ Service Associate ~ Service Desk Associate ~ Social Customization Editor ~ Social Media Community Manager ~ Social Media Manager ~ Social Media Senior Manager ~ Software Engineering Director ~ Sponsorship Director ~ Sponsorship Sales Assistant ~ Sponsorship Sales Director ~ Sponsorship Sales Representative ~ Sponsorship Sales Specialist ~ Sponsorship Services Coordinator ~ Sports Authentic Manager ~ Sport Business Management Faculty ~ Business Systems Analyst ~ Sports Career Counselor ~ Sports Director ~ Sports Editor ~ Sports Management Manager ~ Sports Marketing Director ~ Sports Media Sales Professional ~ Sports/Non-Sports Grader ~ Sports Performance Specialist ~ Sports Program Associate ~ Sports Senior Editor ~ Sports Site Manager ~ Stadium Assistant Manager ~ Stadium Events Assistant Manager ~ Staff Accountant ~ Strategic Account Manager ~ Strategic Partnerships Coordinator ~ Strategic

Planning Manager (Sports) ~ Store Logistics Manager ~ Studio Coordinator ~ Student Operator ~ Talent Acquisition – Vice President ~ Team Sales Representative ~ Technical Operations Cloud Engineer ~ Technical Project Manager ~ Technical Specialist ~ Television Broadcast Associate ~ Temp Sales Associate ~ Territory Sales Manager ~ Ticket and Group Sales Trainee ~ Ticket Operations Manager ~ Ticket Operations Representative ~ Ticket Operator ~ Ticket Package Sales Manager ~ Ticket Sales Account Executive ~ Ticket Sales and Service Manager ~ Ticket Sales Assistant ~ Ticket Sales Executive ~ Ticket Sales – Sales Representative ~ Ticket Sales & Service Coordinator ~ Ticket Sales Manager ~ Tournament Operations Assistant ~ Trackman Operator ~ Treasury Coordinator ~ Treasury & Payroll Accountant ~ Trip Design Manager ~ Truck Driver ~ User Acquisition Manager ~ Vice-President – Analytics & Business Intelligence ~ Video-Board Operator ~ Video Editor ~ Video Editor/Producer ~ Videographer/Editor ~ Video Manager ~ Video Producer & Editor ~ Video Production Associate ~ VIP Services Coordinator ~ Web Analytics Manager ~ Web-based Editor ~ Web Content Editor ~ Wellness & Sports Program Director ~ Wholesale Marketing Coordinator ~ Women's Brand Marketing Director ~ Youth & Services Senior Manager of Finance ~ Youth Camp Site Technical Director ~ Youth Sports Prospector ~ Youth Training Programs Coach.

STUDENT AND STUDENT-ATHLETE PLAN B BOOK
ALL STUDENTS, AND PARTICULARLY, STUDENT-ATHLETES, "DO YOU HAVE A PLAN B?

Professional Occupation Questionnaire for Student Academic & Career Developmental Exposure

Name: Milona A Wall

Your Current Job Title and/or the Job You're Most Known for Participating: Chairman of the Board of Directors, Ozanam, Inc. 2011- current
Number of Years in Current Position or Number of Years in the Position You're Most Known for Participating: 8 years
List the Previous Job Titles You've Had: Chairman of the Board of Directors, Ozanam, Inc. 2011- current, Board of Directors 2010-2011, Teacher PPS- 1973- 2008 (35 years) (Restructuring Coordinator, Instructional Teacher Leader: English and Team, Cheerleading Coach)
List College Major(s), Master's Degree(s), Doctoral Degree(s): Bachelor of Science in Education: Duquesne University,
M.Ed.: University of Pittsburgh

1. **Who inspired you the most?** My parents were my motivators who inspired me.

2. **What motivated you during the pursuit of your career?** My desire and passion to reach my goals are what motivated me, not only as an African American in my late sixties but as the last child in my family. It was vital that I received my degree.

3. **Who or what influenced you to achieve your goal(s) as a professional?**

   Again, my family had a great deal of influence, and yet, by grace, there was a built-in desire for me to attain my goals.

4. **What goal(s) did you set for yourself in attempting to reach your career aspiration(s)?**

   To earn a degree in education and to help youngsters were goals I planned to achieve. After changing from Liberal Arts to Education, I decided that the best way for me to help others, upfront and personal, was to become a teacher. Therefore, I worked with youngsters that looked like me. Hence, my goal was to earn my degree and work in the community.

5. **What were your greatest strengths that you executed as a professional within your career?** My greatest strengths as a professional have been obtaining knowledge, exhibiting leadership skills, respecting other people and expressing the passion I needed within my career.

6. **What most challenged you during your journey to becoming the professional in your occupation?** I was challenged most in my career through the following; the political aspect: texts, system constraints, and fishbowl concept.

7. **How did you manage your weaknesses within your occupation?** I managed my weaknesses by becoming more creative within my occupation.

8. **How important was time management in performing well on your job?** Time management is important. However, when working with youngsters, there are points when you must be flexible.

9. **How much of your educational background factored into obtaining success in your field of work?** My educational background factored considerably in obtaining success in my field of work.

10. **What was your greatest accomplishment as a professional?** My greatest accomplishments are as follows: seeing former students and them remembering you, the smiles and excitement they still have when talking about their time with you, remembering/reciting a class poem or activity that has stuck with them over the years, the hugs, and the thanks!

11. **Why did you or do you work?** I believe people work, because each of us has a calling, and finding it is a true blessing!

12. **What did you or do you value most about your occupation?** What I value most about my occupation is the fact that there is no ego, only respect.

13. **Please feel free to list any future projects you are working on you'd like to promote to list in this Plan B Book:** Future Projects: Ozanam, Inc. endeavors: ASP, STEM, HS Credit Repair, Strength & Conditioning, Breakfast Club, Basketball League, Summer Camp, College Visits, OYBLConference, ASPIRE, African American Legends, Entrepreneur, Role Models, just to name a few.

STUDENT AND STUDENT-ATHLETE PLAN B BOOK
ALL STUDENTS, AND PARTICULARLY, STUDENT-ATHLETES, "DO YOU HAVE A PLAN B?

Professional Occupation Questionnaire for Student Academic & Career Developmental Exposure

Name: Bartina L. Edwards

Your Current Job Title and/or the Job You're Most Known for Participating: Attorney & Co-owner of CP3 Paradigm LLC, a workplace equity company
Number of Years in Current Position or Number of Years in the Position You're Most Known for Participating: 14 years as an attorney
List the Previous Job Titles You've Had: Banking professional, Business Owner/Entrepreneur: owned & managed staffing agency, owned & managed a consulting and strategic firm, owned a turnkey marketing firm
List College Major(s), Master Degree(s), Doctoral Degree(s): Graduated with a double major in French and Business Administration from the College of Charleston, received Juris Doctor from the school of law at the North Carolina Central University School of Law

1. **Who inspired you the most?** My grandmother provided me with the most inspiration.

2. **What motivated you during the pursuit of your career?** My daughter and the need to succeed at something that I had a passion for were the sources of my motivation.

3. **Who or what influenced you to achieve your goal(s) as a professional?** The internal desire I had inside of me, influenced me.

4. **What goal(s) did you set for yourself in attempting to reach your career aspiration(s)?** To complete and succeed at what was placed before me, in order, to attain the end result of becoming whatever it was that I was seeking at the moment were the goals I set for myself.

5. **What were your greatest strengths that you executed as a professional within your career?** Focus, discipline, and resilience were my greatest strengths.

6. **What most challenged you during your journey to becoming the professional in your occupation?** My biggest obstacle I encountered was attempting to put my ego and social definitions aside. The ability to learn that I cannot always be right, and to "stay woke" to the things that can be "minefields" are the challenges I experienced during my career. This is an ongoing challenge for me on my journey.

7. **How did you manage your weaknesses within your occupation?** I managed my weakness by growing from my experiences.

8. **How important was time management in performing well on your job?** Time management is extremely important.

9. **How much of your educational background factored into obtaining success in your field of work?** Having an educational background geared toward your career is totally necessary.

10. **What was your greatest accomplishment as a professional?** Identifying, seeing and obtaining opportunities were my greatest accomplishments. You will always be okay if you see the opportunity in everything.

11. **Why did you or do you work?** I work to fulfill my purpose of helping people which, in turn, helps me socially, financially/economically, spiritually and emotionally to be the best me I can be.

12. **What did you or do you value most about your occupation?** Freedom and autonomy are what I value most about my occupation.

13. **Future projects:** As a co-owner of CP3 Paradigm, LLC, the company promotes equity in the workplace by changing the paradigm through aligning the individual and the company.

COLLEGE JOBS

Account Executive ~ Adjunct Lecturer Professor – Health ~ Physical Education and Recreation ~ Assistant Business Manager ~ Assistant Director of Athletic Facilities and Event Operations ~ Assistant Professor in Coaching ~ Assistant Professor – Department of Physical Therapy ~ Sport Recreation & Fitness Administration ~ Assistant Athletic Director for Marketing ~ Assistant Athletic Trainer – Baseball ~ Assistant Athletic Trainer – Football. Assistant Athletic Trainer – Men's Soccer ~ Assistant Athletic Trainer – Softball ~ Assistant Athletic Trainer – Volleyball ~ Assistant Athletic Trainer - Women's Soccer ~ Assistant Cross-Country and Track and Field Coach (Distance) ~ Assistant Director for Marketing ~ Assistant Director of Compliance ~ Assistant Human Performance Coach ~ Assistant Media Production Coordinator ~ Assistant Professor – Health and Kinesiology ~ Assistant Professor – Health & Physical Education ~ Assistant Professor of Kinesiology ~ Assistant Sports Performance Coach (Baseball) ~ Assistant Sports Performance for Olympic Sports ~ Assistant Sports Performance Coach (Men's Soccer) ~ Assistant Ticket Manager ~ Assistant Track and Field Coach (Hurdles) ~ Assistant Track and Field Coach (Sprint and Relays) ~ Assistant Track and Field Coach (Throws) ~ Assistant Women's Ice Hockey Coach ~ Assistant Women's LaCrosse Coach ~ Associate Athletic Director for Compliance and Student-Athlete Development ~ Associate Athletic Director for Marketing ~ Associate Athletic Director for Media Relations ~ Associate Athletic Director for Media Relations – Baseball ~ Associate Athletic Director for Media Relations – Football ~ Associate Athletic Director for Media Relations – Golf ~ Associate Athletic Director for Media Relations – Men's Basketball ~ Associate Athletic Director for Media Relations – Men's Soccer ~ Associate Athletic Director for Media Relations – Volleyball ~ Associate Athletic Director for Media Relations – Women's Basketball

~ Associate Athletic Director for Media Relations – Women's Soccer ~ Associate Athletic Director for Media Relations – Women's Tennis ~ Associate Athletic Director for Ticket and Facility Operations ~ Associate Director of Basketball Operations ~ Associate Head Athletic Trainer - Men's Basketball ~ Associate Head Athletic Trainer - Women's Basketball ~ Athletic Academic Administrative Assistant ~ Athletic Academic Associate Coordinator ~ Athletic Academic Associate Director ~ Athletic Academic Associate Director/Transitions & Awards Coordinator ~ Athletic Academic Associate Director/Tutor Coordinator ~ Athletic Academic Director ~ Athletic Academic Graduate Assistant ~ Athletic Foundation Assistant Director of the Annual Fund ~ Athletic Foundation Associate Executive Director ~ Athletic Foundation Executive Administrative Assistant ~ Athletic Foundation Gift Analyst ~ Athletic Trainer – Cheerleading ~ Baseball Administrative Assistant ~ Baseball Assistant Coach ~ Baseball Head Coach ~ Baseball Student Assistant Coach ~ Baseball Student Manager ~ Baseball Volunteer Assistant Coach ~ Business Office Assistant ~ Cheerleading Coach ~ College Conference Channels Producer ~ Dance Coach ~ Deputy Athletic Director ~ Deputy Athletic Director for External Affairs ~ Director of Athletic Bands ~ Director of Athletic Facilities and Event Operations ~ Director of Athletic Training - Head Football Athletic Trainer ~ Director of Baseball Operations ~ Director of Compliance ~ Director of Equipment Operations (Football) ~ Director of Football Operations ~ Director of Information Technology ~ Director of Olympic Sports Equipment Operations ~ Director of Sports Performance for Men's Basketball ~ Director of Sports Performance for Olympic Sports and Women's Basketball ~ Director of Student-Athlete Development ~ Director of Ticket Sales ~ Director of Track and Field and Cross Country ~ Executive Assistant to the Athletic Director ~ Executive Associate Athletic Director ~ Executive Director of Athletic Foundation ~ Exercise Physiology Professor ~ Faculty Lecturer (Kinesiology & Athletic Training) ~ Football Assistant Head Coach/Safeties Coach ~ Football Co-

Defensive Coordinator/Cornerbacks Coach ~ Football
Defensive Coordinator/Linebackers Coach ~ Football
Defensive Ends Coach/Recruiting Coordinator ~ Football
Defensive Tackles Coach ~ Football Director of Player
Development ~ Football Graduate Assistant ~ Football Head
Coach ~ Football Offensive Coordinator ~ Football Run-
Game Coordinator; Offensive Line Coach ~ Football Running
Backs Coach ~ Football Special Teams Coordinator/Receivers
Coach ~ Football Tight Ends Coach ~ Football Video
Coordinator ~ Full Time Day & Evening Faculty – Exercise
& Sport Science ~ Full-Time Faculty Kinesiology & Sport
Science Coordinator ~ Full-Time Faculty Kinesiology ~ Full-
Time Instructor (Physical Education and Health Departments)
~ Full-Time Instructor for Functional Gross Anatomy
Lecturer ~ Full-Time Program Coordinator-Kinesiology ~
General Manager of Sports Properties ~ Group Sales Account
Executive ~ Head Coach Cross-Country/Assistant Track and
Field Coach ~ Head Football Strength and Conditioning
Coach ~ Head Track & Field Coach ~ Hospitality Account
Executive ~ Insurance Specialist ~ Kinesiology Instructor and
Director of Human Performance Laboratories ~ Kinesiology
Professor ~ Lifetime Fitness Activity Course Coordinator ~
Marketing Assistant ~ Media Sales Service Executive ~
Media Production Coordinator ~ Membership Sales Account
Executive ~ Men's Basketball Assistant Coach ~ Men's
Basketball Director of Player Development ~ Men's
Basketball Director of Scouting ~ Men's Basketball Graduate
Assistant Coach ~ Men's Basketball Head Coach ~ Men's
Golf Assistant Head Coach ~ Men's Golf Head Coach ~
Men's Soccer Administrative Assistant ~ Men's Soccer
Associate Coach/Goalkeepers Coach ~ Men's Soccer
Associate Head Coach/Recruiting Coordinator ~ Men's Soccer
Head Coach ~ Men's Tennis Assistant Coach ~ Men's Tennis
Head Coach ~ Part Time Day & Evening Faculty – Exercise
& Sport Science ~ Part-Time Faculty Kinesiology & Sport
Science Coordinator ~ Part-Time Faculty Kinesiology ~ Part-
Time Instructor (Physical Education and Health Departments)
~ Part-Time Instructor for Functional Gross Anatomy

Lecturer ~ Part-Time Program Coordinator-Kinesiology ~ Physical Conditioning Professor ~ Physical Education Instructor ~ Physical Therapy Assistant Instructor ~ Senior Associate Athletic Director of Football ~ Softball Administration Assistant ~ Softball Assistant Coach ~ Softball Assistant Coach/Recruiting Coordinator ~ Softball Head Coach ~ Softball Student Assistant Coach ~ Softball Volunteer Assistant Coach ~ Sports Account Executive ~ Sports & Health Science Program Director ~ Sports and Human Performance Faculty ~ Sports Properties Partner Service Coordinator ~ Sports Properties Senior Account Executive ~ Professor of Biomechanics (Department of Movement Arts) ~ Sport Management & Wellness ~ Sports Psychologist ~ Strength Training Professor ~ Ticketing Assistant ~ Ticket Sales Account Executive ~ Ticket Sales and Service Account Executive ~ Ticket Sales Associate General Manager ~ Ticket Sales Representative ~ Track and Field Athletic Trainer ~ Track and Field Sports Psychologist ~ Volleyball Assistant Coach ~ Volleyball Head Coach ~ Volleyball Sports Psychologist ~ Volleyball Volunteer Assistant Coach ~ Volunteer Assistant Track and Field Coach ~ Women's Basketball Assistant Coach ~ Women's Basketball Assistant Coach/Recruiting Coordinator ~ Women's Basketball Assistant Head Coach ~ Women's Basketball Director of Operations ~ Women's Basketball Director of Program Development ~ Women's Basketball Head Coach ~ Women's Basketball Video Coordinator ~ Women's Golf Assistant Head Coach ~ Women's Golf Head Coach ~ Women's Ice Hockey Head Coach ~ Women's LaCrosse Head Coach ~ Women's Soccer Administrative Assistant ~ Women's Soccer Assistant Coach ~ Women's Soccer Goalkeeper Coach ~ Women's Soccer Head Coach ~ Women's Tennis Assistant Coach ~ Women's Tennis Head Coach.

STUDENT AND STUDENT-ATHLETE PLAN B BOOK
ALL STUDENTS, AND PARTICULARLY, STUDENT-ATHLETES, "DO YOU HAVE A PLAN B?

Professional Occupation Questionnaire for Student Academic & Career Developmental Exposure

Name: Mike Hill

Your Current Job Title and/or the Job You're Most Known for Participating: Director of Athletics, UNC Charlotte

Number of Years in Current Position or Number of Years in the Position You're Most Known for Participating: 2 months

List the Previous Job Titles You've Had: Executive Associate Athletics Director, the University of Florida (on staff 24 years at UF)

List College Major(s), Master Degree(s), Doctoral Degree(s): Bachelor of Arts (B.A.) Political Science and Radio/TV/Motion Pictures, the University of North Carolina at Chapel Hill

1. Who inspired you the most?
Jeremy Foley inspired me most who was the former Director of Athletics at the University of Florida.

2. What motivated you during the pursuit of your career?
I've been driven since my high school days to make an impact on college athletics. I have a passion for it, and I have been committed to it my entire career.

3. Who or what influenced you to achieve your goal(s) as a professional?
Jeremy Foley modeled for me the characteristics and traits required to be a successful A.D. I was always motivated by his example. I was, also, impacted by some of the great coaches and student-athletes with whom I've worked, including Billy Donovan, Mike White, Tim Tebow, Abby Wambach, and Bryan Shelton, among many others.

4. What goal(s) did you set for yourself in attempting to reach your career aspiration(s)?
My primary goal was to become an Athletic Director (A.D.) by doing the very best job that I could in the job that I occupied at each stage of my career.

5. What were your greatest strengths that you executed as a professional within your career?
I'm committed to people, and I invest in them. If people understand that you care about them and their happiness, then they are more effective and productive. High emotional intelligence is a must in having a successful career. I, also, believe in being organized and following through, so that, colleagues trust your ability to accomplish things that matter. Lastly, being a strong communicator is crucial to success in any endeavor.

6. What most challenged you during your journey to becoming the professional in your occupation?
It was most challenging, for me, to remain patient for the right opportunity to leave an incredible place like Florida to become an Athletic Director. There were times when I questioned whether or not I would get the chance because there are so many talented administrators who don't. I made the choice to be persistent and believe that it would eventually happen in the right place, and it did. I feel incredibly fortunate.

7. How did you manage your weaknesses within your occupation?
I learned through failure. One of my weaknesses was a lack of self-awareness related to my position. I'm a people person and sometimes naively see myself as "just me," but as you ascend within an organization's structure, people view you through a different lens, whether they should or not. I had to come to terms with that fact and become

more attuned to things that weren't necessarily obvious to me.

8. How important was time management in performing well on your job?
It's essential, and a never-ending battle. I want to be accessible, responsive and involved. But you can't be all things to all people, as there just aren't enough hours in the day to satisfy everyone while also taking care of yourself and your family. It all comes down to prioritization, and it requires the ability to say "no," or "later."

9. How much of your educational background factored into obtaining success in your field of work?
My education at the University of North Carolina helped shape me, certainly. I became a better writer, communicator, and thinker because of my experience there. While I was a student, I gained hands-on experience in the athletic department, which directly impacted my career pursuits.

10. What was your greatest accomplishment as a professional?
I didn't accomplish anything by myself. But I was a part of so many amazing accomplishments at the University of Florida that it's impossible to list them all. That said, some of our proudest accomplishments include negotiating of the nation's largest multi-media contracts, securing a naming rights agreement for the arena, developing a partnership with the College of Journalism to integrate our Gatorvision operation, and building a national championship basketball program. Most importantly, though, I hope I left a legacy at Florida of treating people the right way, with respect and kindness.

11. Why did you or do you work?
It provides immense satisfaction to work together with a team to accomplish something that matters. I can't think of a better environment to experience that than in a college athletics department.

12. What did you or do you value most about your occupation?
People are what I value most about my occupation.

FITNESS JOBS

Accounting Assistant ~ Accounting Director ~ Accounting/Finance Controller ~ Accounting Manager ~ Accounting Senior Supervisor ~ Administration Manager ~ Area Fitness Manager ~ Assistant Athletic Trainer ~ Assistant Director of Marketing ~ Assistant Golf Professional ~ Athletics Chief Financial Officer ~ Athletic Trainer ~ Aqua Fitness Instructor ~ Audience Development Manager ~ Baseball Outdoor Fitness Instructor ~ Category Marketing Director ~ Category Specialist ~ Chief Financial Development Officer ~ Client Services Manager ~ Customer Experience Senior Manager ~ Development Associate Director ~ Digital Marketing Director ~ Digital Product Analytics Manager ~ Director of Accounting ~ Director of Communications ~ Director of Digital Media Services ~ Director of Membership ~ Director of Tickets and Marketing ~ Field Sales Pro ~ Financial Analyst ~ Fitness Director ~ Fitness Manager ~ Fitness Sales Consultant ~ Fitness Service Manager ~ Fitness Specialist ~ Fitness Supervisor ~ Franchise Business Coach ~ General Manager/Fitness Manager ~ Global Media Distribution Director ~ Group Fitness Instructor ~ Gym Teacher ~ Head Athletic Trainer ~ Head Athletic Trainer – Football ~ Head of Sales Operations ~ Head of Sponsorship Sales ~ Health Fitness Program Manager ~ Health Fitness Specialist ~ Human Resources Business Partner ~ Influencer Marketing Director ~ In-Game Social Media Coordinator ~ Inside Sales Associate ~ Inside Sales Consultant ~ Inside Sales Representative ~ Internal Communications Manager ~ Part Time Distribution Specialist ~ Performance Specialist ~ Pilates Instructor ~ Regional Health Fitness Specialist ~ Sales Operations Associate ~ Sales Operations Coordinator ~ Sales Operations Manager ~ Senior Business Systems Analyst ~ Senior Fitness Director ~ Fitness Supervisor ~ Fitness Marketing Senior Manager ~ Learning & Development Specialist ~ Learning Specialist ~ Membership Director ~

Member Engagement Team Leader ~ Member Services Closer ~ Member Services Manager ~ Merchandising Accounting Specialist ~ Merchandising Manager ~ Metabolic Specialist ~ Part-Time Accounting Assistant ~ Payroll Specialist ~ Product Marketing Manager ~ Pro Football Assistant Athletic Trainer ~ Pro Football Assistant Athletic Trainer/Physical Therapist ~ Pro Football Head Athletic Trainer ~ Regional Sales & Operations Manager ~ Retail Marketing Director ~ Retail Sales Specialist ~ Sales Specialist ~ Senior Financial Analyst ~ Senior Merchandising Manager ~ Senior Specialist Retail Marketing ~ Social Media & Content Manager ~ Social Media Manager ~ Social Media Marketing Director ~ Sports Marketing Director ~ Sports Program Associate ~ Strategic Planning Manager ~ Street Team Associate ~ Student Sports Agent Program Specialist ~ Studio Coordinator ~ Tactical Athletic Trainer ~ Team Boot Camp Coach ~ Team Sales Representative ~ Ticket Sales Representative ~ Training Specialist.

STUDENT AND STUDENT-ATHLETE PLAN B BOOK
ALL STUDENTS, AND PARTICULARLY, STUDENT-ATHLETES, "DO YOU HAVE A PLAN B?

Professional Occupation Questionnaire for Student Academic & Career Developmental Exposure

Name: Linda Probst, MAT, ATC, LAT

Your Current Job Title and/or the Job You're Most Known for Participating: Lecturer, Lifetime Fitness Activity Course Coordinator at The University of North Carolina at Charlotte, Kinesiology Department
Number of Years in Current Position or Number of Years in the Position You're Most Known for Participating: 33 years
List the Previous Job Titles You've Had: Lecturer, Teacher, Coach, Licensed Athletic Trainer
List College Major(s), Master Degree(s), Doctoral Degree(s): University of Vermont, Bachelor of Science Degree in Physical Education with a minor in Health Education. Masters of Arts in Teaching from the University of North Carolina at Chapel Hill. Athletic Training curriculum at West Chester University in Pennsylvania.

1. **Who inspired you the most?** My father was my inspiration. He was an outstanding college professor, scientist, inventor, and mentor.

2. **What motivated you during the pursuit of your career?** My motivation came from the passion and love that I have for exercise, movement, sports, injury prevention, and wellness.

3. **Who or what influenced you to achieve your goal(s) as a professional?** I had a gymnastics coach as an undergraduate who inspired me and helped me learn that I could achieve any goal that I set out to reach with hard work and determination.

4. **What goal(s) did you set for yourself in attempting to reach your career aspiration(s)?** I initially wanted to be a teacher and a coach, and then I wanted to become a certified athletic trainer. I eventually knew I wanted to teach at the University level since I grew up in a college town. I knew that to do this, I would have to earn my Master's degree.

5. **What were your greatest strengths that you executed as a professional within your career?** I think my greatest strengths were showing to my students, my passion and love for my profession. I try to inspire students and share my expertise with them in a fun, engaging way while using humor and real-world examples.

6. **What most challenged you during your journey to becoming the professional in your occupation?** Staying up to date on current trends and changes in the profession, via conferences and continuing education.

7. **How did you manage your weaknesses with your occupation?** I try to take advantage of others in my department and professional field to use them as resources and inspirations to assist me when I didn't feel confident in materials that I needed to teach.

8. **How important was time management in performing well on your job?** Time management is extremely important. I feel I learned time management skills in college, and then really put those skills to use as I continued to teach as a mother with two young children. When these skills are learned, it helps to tremendously reduce stress levels.

9. **How much of your educational background factored into obtaining success in your field of work?** I give much of the credit to my success as a professional to past professors I have had in my educational career.

10. **What was your greatest accomplishment as a professional?** I would say my greatest accomplishment has been being able to teach for 44 years and still having a passion for the career while having a true love for working with students.

11. **Why did you or do you work?** I love what I do and it's wonderful to get paid. Obviously, teachers do not go into the field of teaching, in order to become wealthy. I think it is more important to be able to wake up every day and love your job than to be focused on how much money you can make.

12. **What did you or do you value most about your occupation?** I value most of the interactions that I have with my students. They keep me young!

STUDENT AND STUDENT-ATHLETE PLAN B BOOK
ALL STUDENTS, AND PARTICULARLY, STUDENT-ATHLETES, "DO YOU HAVE A PLAN B?

Professional Occupation Questionnaire for Student Academic & Career Developmental Exposure

Name: Ralph Burnett

Your Current Job Title and/or the Job You're Most Known for Participating: Truck Driver

Number of Years in Current Position or Number of Years in the Position You're Most Known for Participating: 67 years

List the Previous Job Titles You've Had: Bowling Alley Employee, Waste Management Professional (Garbage Man), Contractor

List College Major(s), Master Degree(s), Doctoral Degree(s): Studied Education at Fayetteville State University

1. **Who inspired you the most?** Sports and music were two areas of my life that inspired me to excel to the best of my ability in attaining the dreams I dreamed. Sports opened up the door for other things that I wanted to do in life; such as traveling and meeting people from all over the country. It also gave me the "drive" (motivation) in life to persevere to experience better things. Music was, also, a source of enjoyment to me that I began to play in my middle school's band. My desire to travel was satisfied, as well, through learning to play an instrument for the band.

2. **What motivated you during the pursuit of your career?** The motivation that I experienced in the trucking industry, actually, originated during my youth when I would run just about everywhere that I went. Running everywhere gave me the "drive" I would need in life to take on anything that I encountered. Running on a daily basis taught me the lesson of working hard to achieve what I desired, which produced mental and physical endurance. Being involved in physical activities that exercised my body enabled me to be prepared for the physical nature of being a truck driver. Within my profession, I had to be aware of so many things as I drove, which strengthen my mental and physical abilities to perform well on my job. Physical and mental stamina are qualities that I developed within my career which led to the longevity that I've successfully maintained in my occupation all of these years. I, also, benefited from my experience as a truck driver through learning how to talk to different people from different parts of the country to handle various situations. In talking with people on the job, it inspired me to learn how to sell and market an idea, how to negotiate, and how to present the right type of attitude to match the situation I was involved as I encountered different people.

3. **Who or what influenced you to achieve your goal(s) as a professional?**
As I worked as a garbage man, I knew that wasn't going to be sufficient enough for me to reach the financial goals I had set. During this time, my parents got sick, and I had to stay home to work to support the family. So, I went on some delivery runs with my uncle who was a truck driver. As a result, I really liked

it. I began to learn from him all aspects of truck driving, and it brought home enough money to satisfy my dream of traveling and seeing the country as I worked. My uncle's influence gave me a skill set which has lasted my entire adulthood up until this very day.

4. **What goal(s) did you set for yourself in attempting to reach your career aspiration(s)?**
   In the trucking industry, you have to compete with drivers from your own company and other companies in delivering loads, first, so that, you can get unloaded. This will enable you to get off to your next destination. Therefore, I had to set goals with competing against other drivers as a part of my daily schedule to afford myself the opportunity to make the most money I could. So, I had to develop my mind and body to be able to withstand the pressure of the workday, every day. I'm thankful to have gained the wisdom needed to apply my athletic background and experiences to my job, in order to, become more successful within my career. It was important for me to specify goals for the purpose of figuring out how many loads I had to make each day or each month to earn enough money to have my needs met.

5. **What were your greatest strengths that you executed as a professional within your career?**
   My greatest strength was planning how to develop a schedule to deliver my loads on time while making sure that all of my equipment was in good working order. Past athletic and work training contributed to my commitment to hustling and hard work which led to accomplishing what I had to do, to get what I wanted to get. Also, building confidence within your co-workers is vital in cultivating positive relationships

which can lead to building trust, and this is a quality that I learned to execute daily.

6. **What most challenged you during your journey to becoming the professional in your occupation?** Learning from your mistakes is essential to maintaining success as a truck driver. Also, limiting mistakes will lead to securing your job. I knew that handling money was not my strongest skill, so I made sure that I found someone I trusted to tend to my financial needs. Once I got married, I was fortunate to have a wife who was skilled enough to financially care for the entire family's responsibilities as my job had me working out of state. As a truck driver, the constant pressure to deliver goods on time is what challenges you every time you begin a trip for delivery. It requires a lot of courage and "drive" or internal fortitude to be good as an "over-the-road" (long distance) truck driver.

7. **How did you manage your weaknesses within your occupation?** I would go to someone who had experience in the area that I was weak for the purpose of learning from their advice. I would, also, study whatever I was lacking to improve upon what I was weak in to overcome it.

8. **How important was time management in performing well on your job?** Time management is crucial in the trucking industry because the freight you're hauling is just about always scheduled to arrive at a specific time. However, if you can see that you're going to be late, then call the company you're delivering the load. Your customer will appreciate the call. By calling ahead of time, it builds up credibility and shows your responsibility in providing good,

quality customer service. This further develops a relationship with the company that you are serving. Time management is significant for another reason, because if you are running late, then you may be driving too fast which can endanger other drivers, the freight you are hauling and you could get a ticket if you feel you need to drive over the speed limit to make it on time. Therefore, it's wise to account for all of these factors in preparation for each trip that is scheduled.

9. **How much of your educational background factored into obtaining success in your field of work?** Education is important for a truck driver when it comes to record keeping, and filling out your log books to enter the hours you drove while on duty. Education provides the mental blueprint to assist in physically executing the actions required to deliver and unload your merchandise safely and proficiently for your customers.

10. **What was your greatest accomplishment as a professional?** My greatest accomplishments are ongoing because it requires overcoming any obstacle that may arise on your daily delivery route. I was, also, able to work well with others through communication and action which parallels the success of how to execute well on your job, overall. Lastly, respecting the equipment that is placed in your care is critical to transport the materials to the receiver in a manner that is acceptable to them.

11. **Why did you or do you work?** I got involved in the truck business because it was a way to make money and to travel across the United States at someone else's expense. Working was important to me because I was able to provide for my family's needs. I've realized over the years that my work helps to make other people's lives easier while providing some solutions for their transportation and supply needs.

12. **What did you or do you value most about your occupation?** I valued the opportunity truck driving has given me to do some of the things I aspired to accomplish in life. I met many different types of people while being able to see all the continental states, Canada and Mexico at the company's expense. I'm fortunate to have had an enjoyable occupation which allowed me to be financially stable enough to provide for my family's needs. It was important for me to have a job that I could take my children around the country for them to witness life outside of their hometown. My profession has provided the essentials of life for my children, so they could have the best opportunity to succeed in this world.

GRADUATE ASSISTANT JOBS

Academic Support Graduate Assistant ~ Assistant Athletic Trainer Graduate Assistant ~ Associate Director Video Production Graduate Assistant ~ Associate Athletic Director for Internal Relations ~ Athletic Operations Graduate Assistant ~ Communications Graduate Assistant ~ Diving Coach Graduate Assistant ~ Food and Nutrition Editor ~ Football Graduate Assistant ~ Freelance Production Assistant Graduate Assistant ~ Golf Graduate Assistant ~ Graphics Production Assistant ~ Internal Operations ~ Marketing & Promotions Graduate Assistant ~ Media Relations Graduate Assistant ~ Men's & Women's Swim Graduate Assistant Coach ~ Men's Lacrosse Graduate Assistant ~ Men's Soccer Graduate Assistant ~ Men's Volleyball Graduate Assistant ~ Seasonal Video Assistant ~ Sports Information/Game Management Graduate Assistant ~ Summer Marketing & Promotions Crew Graduate Assistants ~ Tennis Coach Graduate Assistant ~ Track & Field Graduate Assistant ~ Triathlon Graduate Assistant Coach ~ Video Production Graduate Assistant ~ Video Production & Multimedia Graduate Assistant ~ Women's Golf Graduate Assistant ~ Women's Lacrosse Graduate Assistant ~ Women's Soccer Graduate Assistant ~ Women's Softball Graduate Assistant ~ Women's Volleyball Graduate Assistant ~ Wrestling Graduate Assistant.

STUDENT AND STUDENT-ATHLETE PLAN B BOOK
ALL STUDENTS, AND PARTICULARLY, STUDENT-ATHLETES, "DO YOU HAVE A PLAN B?

Professional Occupation Questionnaire for Student Academic & Career Developmental Exposure

Name: Robert Craig Poole

Your Current Job Title and/or the Job You're Most Known for Participating: Presently retired, however, I am a volunteer coach with San Diego State University coaching jumper. I, also, serve as a resource consultant with coaches.

Number of Years in Current Position or Number of Years in the Position You're Most Known for Participating: I spent 16 years in public schools, (6 at a junior high and 10 at high school and then 30 years as Head coach/director of the BYU's women track program and as a Professor teaching in the College of Health. I spent four years as the Head Coach/Director of the OTC's track and field program under the direction of the USA Track and Field (USATF) and the United States Olympic Committee (USOC).

List the Previous Job Titles You've Had: I have always been a head coach until retirement, and now as a volunteer assistant coach I am having the time of my life. I really did not know how enjoyable being an assistant could be.

List College Major(s), Master's Degree(s), Doctoral Degree(s): BS and MS degrees from Utah State University: Doctoral degree in Education (Ed.D) from the University of Utah. All degrees in Physical education/ Zoology/physiology/ minor in Special Education. Doctoral degree in Education (Ed.D) in Exercise Science and a minor in Education Administration.

1. **Who inspired you the most?** My father was the inspirer of my direction. He was a coach, and I learned most of what I know from him. He set the example, provided the direction, and counsel. He also told me never to be a coach. He advised me to be a lawyer, dentist, or doctor, but not a coach. So, I prepared for that direction. However, I had a scholarship that required me to get a teaching certificate, and so, I followed in his footsteps. When I did, he counseled me that I needed to be financially able to survive. I needed to have an advanced degree, thus, I needed to complete the list above. This is, also, what drove me to the love of learning and the study of Sport Psychology in the postdoctoral area. Thus, this led me to my university teaching assignment.

2. **What motivated you during the pursuit of your career?** I have always liked sports. My father was an outstanding athlete and coach. I always played sports from my youth until college. During those years my father was my coach even through high school. I was small, but good at what I did. I won several honors that motivated me to continue in this career. I liked winning. Later on, I learned how I wanted to project winning and what it really meant.

3. **Who or what influenced you to achieve your goal(s) as a professional?** I have always believed, and probably, it was instilled in me to get a good education. The more I learned, the more I wanted to learn. I figured that if I knew enough, or had a broader background, then those I coached against, I could beat. I think that has proven to be true to a certain extent,

but this has driven my lifelong journey to continue to read and study anything related to my sport. This helped me do a better job. My postdoctoral work was done in Performance Psychology. Dr. Keith Henschen worked with me for years as a consultant to my teams. His service and input were invaluable in enabling those I worked with to be successful. He, also, influenced my style of coaching and philosophy. Once I learned the biomechanics, physiology, and techniques of my sport, I quickly learned that success was not to be unless you could disseminate that information to your athletes.

4. **What goal(s) did you set for yourself in attempting to reach your career aspiration(s)?** I wanted to be able to provide for my family. With a Bachelor of Science Degree (BS), you did not make enough to have some of the good things of life. I was brought up in a family where my father was a teacher and a coach. We struggled, and he had to find outside work to provide. While living in that type of environment, I decided that I wanted a job that was fun, and that I could work at and be successful full time. If I decided to take something, it has to be with full focus. So, I followed the advice he gave me and pursued advanced degrees, in order to reach that goal. I am so happy that I did. I can truly say that I have been paid full time for having fun in what I do.

5. **What were your greatest strengths that you executed as a professional within your career?** As I evolved as a coach, teacher, and with my background in the sciences, I think that I served as a bridge between the art of coaching and the application of the sciences. I believe that in the programs I have been responsible for, I have been able to weave the sciences into the coaching application. I have created ways for science application to be included in sports through disseminating it to both coaches and athletes. Performance Psychology is imperative to that process of success. There are several learning styles, teaching methods, personality types, hang-ups, and you name it that influence performance. I sometimes joke that a coach needs a toolbox full of wrenches to fix all the "nuts" he/she deals with daily. Having support services in the sciences (especially psychology) aid this process and many times it makes or breaks the process.

6. **What most challenged you during your journey to becoming the professional in your occupation?** I believe that the first steps were the hardest, but looking back perhaps the most rewarding. After finishing my Bachelor of Science (BS), I started a Master's Degree (MS), and I got married at age 23. My first full-time job required me to open a new Junior High School, performing as a full-time Physical Educator and Health teacher. I did all of this while finishing my MS degree. That took a year and a summer. Then, when I was completing my second year of teaching, I looked for a summer job, but I couldn't find one. So, I went back to school and

started a doctoral program. So, teaching full time and going to school was my biggest challenge. I might add I was also coaching full time. This stimulus convinced me, even more, the benefits and rewards of continued education. I needed to polish my skills, in order to, reach the needs of my student-athletes for the purpose of helping them reach their genetic potential.

7. **How did you manage your weaknesses within your occupation?** I tried harder. I reached out to others who had the strengths I needed, and I tried to learn from them. I attended camps, clinics, international conferences, read research/books, and subscribed to as many periodicals as I could. I would read constantly, taking notes, creating ideas, progressions, and developing understandings. I reached out to those coaches successful in the field and visited with them wherever I could. I picked their brain, asked for advice, and bounced ideas off of my dad while trying to tie all strings together until it really made sense. [But] Probably the hardest thing I had to learn was how to work with administrations. We (I) had ideas that I wanted to implement, and it (they) required money. How do you sell it to the administration and convince them to support and buy into what you are doing in a way that will help you be successful? But, most of all, how do you sell the school and the student-athletes with a great experience for them both to benefit? (This is a tough call sometimes depending on the philosophy of the school and the administrator.)

8. **How important was time management in performing well on your job?** Time management is very important. You have to put in the time. But not just putting it in, you have to make the time count both in the job and outside of the job. Time is required for family, community, school, and church. All which help to make you a well-rounded individual and a happy one as well. We cannot just have a "One Track Mind"! We must set priorities and goals, not outcome goals, but process goals. The process determines the outcome, so when the process is right, the outcome will be good. So, all my organization in time was directed toward the process to fill all life demands and areas.

9. **How much of your educational background factored into obtaining success in your field of work?** As you can see from the above, this is of prime importance to me.

10. **What was your greatest accomplishment as a professional?** My greatest accomplishment was to see the student-athletes grow and excel in life. When your process is right, other honors will come your way, and I have had many. I appreciate them all, but the biggest honor for me is when athletes come back and express thanks for the difference I made in their lives.

11. **Why did you or do you work?** I work because I still have fun. It has always been fun.

12. What did you or do you value most about your occupation? I value the association with people who want to be better, who enjoy a challenge and work hard, (dedicated) to achieve the challenge. Coaching is an art form. Coaching helps to mold personalities, and it helps people to better deal with life's challenges. When a person handles success and deals with setbacks, it brings value to the process. Coaches are the conduit to this process.

STUDENT AND STUDENT-ATHLETE PLAN B BOOK
ALL STUDENTS, AND PARTICULARLY, STUDENT-ATHLETES, "DO YOU HAVE A PLAN B?

Professional Occupation Questionnaire for Student Academic & Career Developmental Exposure

Name: Tim O'Riley

Your Current Job Title and/or the Job You're Most Known for Participating: Financial Operations Administrator/Analyst
Number of Years in Current Position or Number of Years in the Position You're Most Known for Participating: 5 years
List the Previous Job Titles You've Had: College/High School/Club Track Coach, Videographer/Cameraman, Financial Analyst, Benefits Specialist, Retention Specialist, Loans Administrator, Data Analyst
List College Major(s), Master Degree(s), Doctoral Degree(s): Bachelor of Arts in English, Bachelor of Science in Business Admin w/ split concentration in Finance/Marketing

1. **Who inspired you the most?** My father, coaches and some professors inspired me most.

2. **What motivated you during the pursuit of your career?** The following motivated me while I pursued my career: being able to do something with my degrees, being able to provide for my wife, building a life and being financially independent.

3. **Who or what influenced you to achieve your goal(s) as a professional?** My professors and professional mentors were very influential to me.

4. **What goal(s) did you set for yourself in attempting to reach your career aspiration(s)?** My goals consisted of obtaining certifications, learning new skills and gaining career-specific experience.

5. **What were your greatest strengths that you executed as a professional within your career?** My strong written and verbal communication skills were critically needed in project correspondences which were my greatest strengths. Recently, I have developed my sideline filming skills at high school football events, which developed into my latest strength.

6. **What most challenged you during your journey to becoming the professional in your occupation?** The constant closing doors, and job instability, most challenged me, but I had to continue to persevere.

7. **How did you manage your weaknesses within your occupation?** I paid attention to what skills were on demand, and I had to work to improve them. So, I tried to diversify the industries where I was trying to work.

8. **How important was time management in performing well on your job?** It was very important, as I was in several environments where things were changing all the time.

9. **How much of your educational background factored into obtaining success in your field of work?** Education somewhat factored into it. Experience is equally important, and certifications don't get enough credit.

10. **What was your greatest accomplishment as a professional?** With no prior business plan writing experience, I single-handedly generated and produced a business plan full of analysis for an engineer to his satisfaction. No one outworked me. It was a group project that I had to take on myself.

11. **Why did you or do you work?** I find dignity in work. I work to provide for myself, and my wife, and to keep my mind active.

12. **What did you or do you value most about your occupation?** The thing I value most is discovering new talents and skills that I wasn't aware that I had.

13. Please feel free to list any future projects you are working on you'd like to promote to list in this Plan B Book: I am a sepsis survivor, and I now have the vision to raise funds to raise sepsis awareness which is a deadly infectious disease that spreads rapidly and kills quickly if left undiagnosed. It's your immune system's abnormal response to an infection or an illness. The Sepsis Alliance is a network for those who like to host events like a 5k road race, volleyball tournament or bowling outing. I would like to host one within a year. Also, as a part-time videographer for "Under the Radar Sports Media" it is possible that I'm filming and exposing potential future professional athletes and even Hall of Famers. I covered the starting quarterback for the South Pointe High Stallions this past season. In the fall of 2018, he will be playing for the Clemson Tigers.

HEALTH & WELLNESS AND NUTRITION JOBS

Concessions Sales Auditor ~ Director of Sports Nutrition ~ Food and Nutrition Editor ~ Health & Wellness Consultant ~ Health Fitness Program Manager ~ Health Fitness Specialist ~ Healthy Athletes Program Manager ~ Metabolic Specialist ~ Nurse's Aide ~ Nutrition Program Coordinator ~ Organic Food Manufacturer ~ Pediatrician ~ Physical Therapist ~ Pro Football Internal Medicine Physician ~ Pro Football Neurosurgery Physician ~ Pro Football Orthopedic Surgery Physician ~ Nutrition Program Coordinator ~ Nutrition Program Lead ~ Regional Director of Food & Beverage ~ Regional Health Fitness Specialist ~ Sports Medicine Associate Athletics Director ~ Sports Nutrition Operations Coordinator ~ Sports Psychologist ~ Sports Scientist ~ Wellness and Sports Program Director ~ Wellness Director.

STUDENT AND STUDENT-ATHLETE PLAN B BOOK
ALL STUDENTS, AND PARTICULARLY, STUDENT-ATHLETES, "DO YOU HAVE A PLAN B?

Professional Occupation Questionnaire for Student Academic & Career Developmental Exposure

Name: Dr. William Sears

Your Current Job Title and/or the Job You're Most Known for Participating: Pediatrician for over 50 years, and he currently is a doctor at his family practice: Sears Family Pediatrics where his sons, Dr. Jim Sears and Dr. Bob Sears are doctors, as well.

Number of Years in Current Position or Number of Years in the Position You're Most Known for Participating: over 50 years

List the Previous Job Titles You've Had: Pediatrician, Professor of Pediatrics at 4 universities: the University of Toronto, University of South Carolina, University of Southern California School of Medicine, the University of California at Irvine School of Medicine. Pediatric training at Harvard Medical School and Toronto Children's Hospital (The world's largest children's hospital).

List College Major(s), Master Degree(s), Doctoral Degree(s): He obtained a Medical Degree, Fellow of the Royal College Pediatricians (FRCP) of Pediatricians in Canada which allows him to practice pediatrics anywhere in the world.

1. **Who inspired you the most?** My mother inspired me the most. After experiencing childhood as an only child being raised by a single mother, it was the strength and hardworking ethic of my mom that gave me the passion to succeed in life. My mom surrounded me with quality male mentors, such as my grandfather.

As I give talks to boys & girls clubs and underprivileged kids, I stress to them the importance that many of their circumstances can't always be changed. However, they can change how they deal with them knowing that their future is their choice. Also, my quality male mentors emphasized to me the significance of the power of positive thinking. They imparted, to me, that your future is under your control, and it is your destiny, not your past.

2. **What motivated you during the pursuit of your career?** I wanted a career where I could experience a lot of joy. Nowadays, the joyous state of mind and feeling that I "coined" in my life is what I call "the Helpers High". The helpers high I define as doing something to help someone else! At the end of the day, I wanted to have done something which would have made a small difference that would have helped someone else and brought some type of joy to their lives by something I said or did. This is why I went into medicine. Therefore, I went into pediatrics to make the most influence over a long period of time in the lives of people beginning at the earliest point of their lives. As a pediatrician, I wanted to be able to steer the parents in the right direction by giving life-enhancing skills, wisdom, and information to their children that could benefit them throughout their lifetime.

3. **Who or what influenced you to achieve your goal(s) as a professional?** I married wisely. I advise young adults when they choose a mate to marry; it is the most important choice they can make in life.

4. **What goal(s) did you set for yourself in attempting to reach your career aspiration(s)?** Personal happiness and satisfaction was a big goal for me to apprehend. So, that is where I set my sights. Unfortunately, I didn't know early on in my young adulthood to make health my hobby. However, as I progressed in my career, I began to realize the enjoyment that I had in doing my job. Thus, it didn't seem like work to me.

5. **What were your greatest strengths that you executed as a professional within your career?** Persistence, motivation, and wanting to play football in high school as one of the smaller kids gave me the drive to be the best I could in what I aimed to achieve. I knew I had to run faster to be successful in getting to the goals I wanted. This mindset led me to become the quarterback of the football team and a captain. Since I had a great desire to play football, I focused on what I could do and I didn't focus on what I couldn't do. As a result, my football experience turned out to be a positive one. I was surrounded by very wise men that helped to guide me during my school years. My mother had me around good mentor like the firemen at the local fire station, local pastors, coaches and Boy Scout leaders who all spoke positivity into my life. A tip that I share with young husbands is that you want to model the type of man you want your daughters to marry.

6. **What most challenged you during your journey to becoming the professional in your occupation?** Financial challenges, juggling family life and work life were the biggest challenges for me along my professional journey. I had to learn that the family had to come first even when work seemed to present itself as the highest priority at the time. It was extremely hard learning to re-prioritize the family/work dynamic in my life. The turning point came in my life when I was offered a job at the largest children's hospital in the world, but I turned it down because it would have taken me further away from my family. My family's success was more important than the success of my career. This turned out to be the number one key in the growth of maturity for me early on in my adulthood. It's, also, really important to surround yourself around wise people and to be humble enough to listen and learn from them. We, as a society, are wiser people because we have made mistakes and if we learn from these mistakes. We should pass on our experiences to the youth, then, in turn, this can save the youth from making the same mistakes themselves.

7. **How did you manage your weaknesses within your occupation?** I tried to keep up on the latest research and learning from other doctors who assisted me in becoming more knowledgeable of the things I needed to enhance within my career. Studying and working on writing books helped me to gain more understanding which benefited me in strengthening those areas that needed improvement.

8. **How important was time management in performing well on your job?** Time management was very important to me. I love to be punctual because I get to enjoy the day more and I am less stressed. Fortunately, I have been able to master this skill.

9. **How much of your educational background factored into obtaining success in your field of work?** It factored into my success of about 50%. I learned most about working after I graduated while I was working within my career. I believe education is the first step towards opening the door that leads to the opportunity that can produce success.

10. **What was your greatest accomplishment as a professional?** My greatest professional accomplishments are as follows: being honored to be on the cover of Time magazine in May 2012 for family health contributions, receiving feedback from others of how I have helped them, and authoring 47 books. My personal accomplishments are as follows: I've been married for 52 years, fathering 8 children and creating the Dr. Sears Wellness Institute to inspire healthy living around the world. (I, David Burnett, who is the author of this book, am a graduate of Dr. Sears' Wellness Institute)

11. **Why did you or do you work?** I don't retire because; I love kids and helping parents. I, also, get enjoyment and personal satisfaction in giving people what they need to have a better quality of life.

12. What did you or do you value most about your occupation? My job is so gratifying because it gives you the most joy and personal reward. Poor health is the #1 problem in America, and my occupation is a service that can positively influence poor health to better outcomes.

13. Please feel free to list any future projects you are working on you'd like to promote to list in this Plan B Book:
Dr. Sears Wellness Institute is working on a brain health program to benefit all people and all ages.

Do you have any additional comments to encourage our youth? To all the youth, make health your hobby, meditate more and agitate less, and have an attitude of gratitude.

STUDENT AND STUDENT-ATHLETE PLAN B BOOK
ALL STUDENTS, AND PARTICULARLY, STUDENT-ATHLETES, "DO YOU HAVE A PLAN B?

Professional Occupation Questionnaire for Student Academic & Career Developmental Exposure

Name: Marvella Brown

Your Current Job Title and/or the Job You're Most Known for Participating: Physical Therapist

Number of Years in Current Position or Number of Years in the Position You're Most Known for Participating: 43 years

List the Previous Job Titles You've Had: Nurse's aide, Chief Physical Therapist, Senior Physical Therapist for the rehab center, Supervising Physical Therapist at a hospital over 200 patients, Physical therapist for special needs students for the Pittsburgh Public School System.

List College Major(s), Master Degree(s), Doctoral Degree(s): Bachelor of Science in Physical Therapy, Obtained many Certifications in Physical Therapy.

1. **Who inspired you the most?** My mother and father inspired me most because they insisted that I was to pursue a good education. My father's elbow was crushed when I was 8 or 9 years old, and I tried to massage his arm to help make him feel better. As a result of that experience, I have had a passion to help better improve the way people feel and move.

2. **What motivated you during the pursuit of your career?** I was motivated during my career when I was in high school working as a nurse's aide. As a result, I became passionate about helping people with their health which led me into the health profession.

3. **Who or what influenced you to achieve your goal(s) as a professional?**
My best friend, Sylvia, encouraged me to keep working hard throughout my college years to do everything I needed to do to earn my degree in physical therapy. I, also, had a fellow physical therapist who was influential to me. He emphasized the importance of caring for the patient, first, which allowed me to learn from his example. My mom instructed me to give good care to people no matter what. She, also, told me not to be concerned about outside things or personal things which may affect my performance. She said to always take care of the patient's needs, in order, to ensure their well-being is satisfied. My teacher, Ms. Kelly, advised me that I would have to develop a tough skin because people are going to test you. She said they'll try you and discourage you. My parents consistently encouraged me to pursue my goals in life, especially education. While working one day on the job, I noticed a student who had a lack of range of motion and mobility in school. I decided to take the job as a physical therapist to help improve his quality of life. This role influenced and impacted me so much that it led me to assist other students with their mobility, scholastic aptitude, and basic needs.

4. **What goal(s) did you set for yourself in attempting to reach your career aspiration(s)?**

   I needed financial assistance, so I set a goal to get a scholarship for college, and fortunately, I achieved. I wanted to work on the weekends to help pay for my college needs. Once I became a physical therapist, my friends, parents, and teachers encouraged me to succeed by getting the right continued education classes needed to improve upon my skills. After completing my additional certification classes, it allowed me to attain my goals which enabled me to become the best health professional I could.

5. **What were your greatest strengths that you executed as a professional within your career?**

   My patients used to say to me your, "My marvelous Marvella" for the physical therapy assistance I provided them. My greatest strength was attributed to being humble. I tried to give all my patients the best care that I could. Another strength I strived to execute each day was to be nice, and to live by the adage, "It doesn't cost too much to be nice." I also learned to view each patient as a total person or full unit working altogether. I saw each patient as a person, and not by the disabled limb or disability that the patient was encountering. I, also, had to manage their psyches, many times, alongside their physical challenges. So, I learned that we need to understand people as much as we can, mentally and emotionally. This truly helps the whole person receive their best care. To be a proficient physical therapist, I believed it was important to always finish my paperwork each day. I came to know that in the medical field, you can't play with people's lives.

6. **What most challenged you during your journey to becoming the professional in your occupation?** Some co-workers may have unfair thoughts or actions brought against you on the job undeservingly. However, if you work hard and work with integrity, then things will work themselves out for you. In the physical therapy field during this time in society, jobs weren't readily available to women, lower level economic applicants and certain people within certain ethnic groups when compared to men, the affluent, and the majority ethnic group.

7. **How did you manage your weaknesses within your occupation?** Early on in my career, I didn't work much with children. However, my supervisor saw that I was improving their health issues. She, also, encouraged me to continue getting additional education through attending workshops to enhance the level of care I could administer. I knew I had a weakness writing written assignments in college, but my best friend Sylvia would help me write them. As a result, I learned to write the correct way.

8. **How important was time management in performing well on your job?** Time management was really important. For most of my early career, my paperwork was handwritten. However, when technology advanced in society, the physical therapy field introduced computer reporting as the preferred method to submit our reports. Due to my unfamiliarity with computers, I had to adjust my time to allow for learning how to use a computer. So, after I treated my patients, I spent more time with co-workers to receive tutoring from them to learn how to use a

computer. Sometimes, I had to stay later at work to finish this new way of reporting. Therefore, you have to be able to assess a situation and find the time to work on a solution.

9. **How much of your educational background factored into obtaining success in your field of work?** All of my courses in college helped to give me a keener sense of insight and understanding, in which, I used to become a better overall physical therapist. This enabled me to apply new techniques more effectively that I received from additional education courses at Johns Hopkins University Training Center.

10. **What was your greatest accomplishment as a professional?** I had a feeling a patient had a misdiagnosis by the doctors, and as a result, I asked the doctor if it seemed like it could be something else besides what was originally diagnosed. So, the doctor did more testing and found out it was actually something else other than the original diagnosis. My suggestion helped the patient to finally get the health relief he needed. Another kid was so depressed he really aged, and I knew I had to do something to make him happier. After I developed exercises focused on happiness, his appearance became more youthful. These two situations were examples of the effective and helpful accomplishments that I was blessed enough to extend to my patients.

11. **Why did you or do you work?** I appreciated each day I had an opportunity to work. It was out of necessity to provide for my family as a single parent that I worked. I committed myself to work every day, and thankfully, I really enjoyed my occupation.

12. What did you or do you value most about your occupation? I valued that my patients saw they were getting what they needed, and they were benefiting from my assistance. Sometimes, I talked to my patients after physical therapy was over, because they may not have had family or many friends in their lives. Therefore, I appreciated being a factor in providing essential needs for the betterment of their lives.

13. What advice would you give your school-aged self as a student preparing for a future career? I would advise all students, including my younger self, to check out what classes you would need to study in school, like physics and chemistry; to be better equipped to succeed as a physical therapist. Get an advisor who can help you fill out an application for a college scholarship. As a student, look into more than one field of study to make yourself more appealing to the job market. Prepare yourself for post-college continued education, and seek out an older physical therapist or even other professionals in different fields to mentor you. The better equipped you are, then the better you will perform on your job. Know your weaknesses and improve on them. Never give up your dream, and you can succeed if you don't give up. Everyone has been given at least one talent, so, find out what it is and go after it, relentlessly.

INTERNSHIPS

Academy Intern, Account Manager ~ Accounting Intern ~ Administration Intern ~ Advertising Sales Intern ~ Archives Intern ~ Assistant Football Coach Intern ~ Assistant Sales Manager Intern ~ Associate Director Video production ~ Athlete Leadership Intern ~ Athlete & Program Development Intern ~ Athletic Apparel Graphic Design Intern ~ Athletic Apparel Sales Intern ~ Athletic Communication Intern ~ Athletic Facilities and Game Operations Intern ~ Athletic Trainer Intern ~ Athletics Media Relations Director ~ Athletics Operations Intern ~ Athletics Ticket Office Intern ~ Athletic Training Intern ~ Baseball Scouting Intern ~ Basketball Analytics Intern ~ Basketball Operations Intern ~ Basketball Scout Intern ~ Boston Baseball Ambassador Intern ~ Brand Marketing Intern ~ Branded Attractions Intern ~ Broadcast/Public Relations Intern ~ Business Analytics Intern ~ Business Development Intern ~ Charity Fundraising Intern ~ City League Director ~ Client Services Intern ~ Client Strategy Intern ~ Club House Assistant Intern ~ Club House Manager Intern ~ Communication Intern ~ Communication/Marketing Intern ~ Community Affairs Intern ~ Community Outreach Intern ~ Community & Sponsor Services Intern ~ Community Relations Intern ~ Community Relations Summer Intern ~ Consumer Marketing Intern ~ Content Development Intern ~ Content Development Social Media Intern ~ Content Team Intern ~ Content Writer Intern ~ Corporate Sales Intern ~ Creative Services Intern ~ Design & Graphics Intern ~ Design Intern with Marketing ~ Design (Outdoor) Intern ~ Development Intern ~ Development Assistant Intern ~ Digital Marketing Intern ~ Digital Media Content Intern ~ Digital Video Coordinator Intern ~ Director of Legal Intern ~ Director of Soccer Operations ~ Donor Relations Intern ~ Ecommerce Intern ~ Editorial Intern ~ Emerging Business Intern ~ Engineering

Intern ~ Event Management Assistant Intern ~ Event Management Intern ~ Event Operations Intern ~ Events and Operations Intern ~ Events Intern ~ Events Operations Coordinator Intern ~ Facility Operations Intern ~ Fall Production Intern (Assists production staff in research ~ video acquisition ~ field remote planning ~ logging interviews & feature segments) ~ Family Services Intern ~ Finance Intern ~ Fitness Intern ~ Flash Programmer Intern ~ Football Communications Intern ~ Footwear Design Intern ~ Foundation/Community Relations Intern ~ Game Day Intern ~ Global Brand Marketing Intern ~ Global Partnerships Intern ~ Graphic Design Intern ~ Grassroots Events Baseball Intern ~ Group Sales Intern ~ Group Ticket/Sales Intern ~ Guest Services Intern ~ Health Intern ~ Health Fitness Intern ~ Healthy Athletes Intern ~ Hospitality Intern ~ Human Resources Intern ~ Human Resources Summer Intern ~ Indoor Athletic Facilities Intern ~ Industrial Design Intern ~ Information Technology Intern ~ Inside Sales Intern ~ Intern Athletic Trainer - Cross Country/Track & Field ~ Intern Athletic Trainer – Football ~ Intern Athletic Trainer – Tennis ~ Intern Writer ~ Junior Sales Academy Intern ~ Junior Analyst Summer Intern ~ Law Enforcement Intern ~ Legal Intern ~ Marketing & Communications Intern ~ Marketing & Game Day Operations Intern ~ Marketing & Public Relations Intern ~ Marketing Assistant Intern ~ Marketing Coordinator Intern ~ Marketing Intern ~ Marketing Manager Intern ~ Marketing Operations Intern ~ Mascot Intern ~ Master Control Operator ~ Materials Design Intern ~ Media Manager Intern ~ Media/PR Coordinator Intern ~ Media Production Intern ~ Media Relations Cross Country Intern ~ Media Relations Intern ~ Media Relations Softball Intern ~ Media Relations Track & Field Intern ~ Merchandise Sales Intern ~ Multimedia Intern ~ News Intern ~ Office Administration Intern ~ Official Scorekeeper Intern ~ On-Air Promotions Intern ~ Operations Intern ~ Operations/Production Intern ~ Operations and Strategy Intern ~ Organizational Development Intern ~ Performance Dietitian Intern ~ Performance Spec Intern ~ Photo/Video Intern ~ Photographer Intern ~ Player

Outreach Intern ~ Podcast Intern ~ Post Editor Intern ~ Pro Baseball Content Entry Specialist Intern ~ Production Intern ~ Production Team Intern ~ Product Support Partner Care Intern ~ Pro Football Content Entry Specialist Intern ~ Pro Football Club Events Intern ~ Pro Football Digital Commerce Intern ~ Pro Football Equipment Intern ~ Pro Football Fulfillment and Logistics Intern ~ Pro Football IT Intern ~ Pro Football Marketing Intern ~ Pro Football Partnership Activation Intern ~ Pro Football Photography Intern ~ Pro Football Project Assistant Intern ~ Pro Football Public Relations/Media Intern ~ Pro Football Scouting Intern ~ Pro Football Social Media Intern ~ Pro Football Social Media Marketing Intern ~ Pro Football Spanish Content Intern ~ Pro Football TV Intern ~ Pro Football Video/Production Intern ~ Pro Football Volunteer & Social Media Intern ~ Program Intern ~ Project Unify Intern ~ Pro Sports Sponsorship Compliance Intern ~ Pro Sports Tournament Operations Intern ~ Public Relations Intern ~ Public Relations Intern and Marketing Intern ~ Retail Allocator Intern ~ Retail Buying Intern ~ Retail Marketing Intern ~ Sales Assistant Intern ~ Sales Intern ~ Sales and Marketing Graduate Intern ~ Sales & Service Intern ~ Sales & Service Team Intern ~ Sales/Media Relations Intern ~ Seasonal Game-day Intern ~ Senior Soccer Scout Intern ~ Shows/Video Intern ~ Soccer Scout Intern ~ Social Media Coordinator ~ Social Design Intern ~ Social Media & Content Manager ~ Social Media Intern ~ Social Media & Graphic Design Intern ~ Social Media Marketing Associate ~ Social Media Manager ~ Social Stories Intern ~ Softgoods Design Intern ~ Software Development Intern ~ Special Event & Hospitality Intern ~ Special Events Intern ~ Special Events & LETR Intern ~ Special Events Social Strategy Intern ~ Sponsor Activation Intern ~ Sponsorship and Development Intern ~ Sponsorship Compliance Intern ~ Sponsorship Summer Intern ~ Sports and Fitness Intern ~ Sports Broadcaster Intern ~ Sport Business Development Intern ~ Sports Broadcaster Intern ~ Sports Information Director Intern ~ Sports Information Intern ~ Sports Intern ~ Sports Management/Marketing Intern ~ Sports Marketing Intern ~

Sports Marketing Tennis Intern ~ Sports & Programs Intern ~ Sports Research Intern ~ Sports Social Media Intern ~ Stadium Operations Intern ~ Stadium Operations Associate Intern ~ Strategic Planning Intern ~ Student-Athlete Development Intern ~ Summer Camp Intern ~ Summer Creative Strategy Intern ~ Summer IT Intern ~ Summer Ticket Sales Intern ~ Team Account Executive Intern ~ Team & Venue Services Intern ~ Tech Intern ~ Ticket Office Intern ~ Ticket Office Game Day Intern ~ Ticket Office Summer Intern ~ Ticket Operations Intern ~ Ticket Operations/Finance Intern ~ Ticket Sales & Operations Assistant Intern ~ Ticket Sales Assistant Intern ~ Tournament Liaison Intern ~ UnderGrad Media Relations Intern ~ Unified Sports Management Intern ~ Unified School Intern ~ Video Content Production Intern ~ Video Intern ~ Video Editing Intern ~ Video/Photo Production Intern ~ Video Production Associate Intern ~ Video Production Coordinator Intern ~ Video Production Intern ~ Video Streaming Coordinator ~ Video Storytelling Intern ~ Volunteer & Social Media Intern ~ Volunteer Operations Intern ~ Volunteer Program Intern ~ Warehouse and Logistics Intern ~ Website Coordinator Intern ~ Wholesale Business Planning Intern ~ Women In Sports Intern ~ Young Athletes Intern ~ Youth Development Intern ~ Youth Sports Director Intern ~ Youth Sports Intern ~ Youth Sports Network Intern ~ Youth Sports Prospector Intern.

STUDENT AND STUDENT-ATHLETE PLAN B BOOK
ALL STUDENTS, AND PARTICULARLY, STUDENT-ATHLETES, "DO YOU HAVE A PLAN B?

Professional Occupation Questionnaire for Student Academic & Career Developmental Exposure

Name: David Burnett

Your Current Job Title and/or the Job You're Most Known for Participating: Business Owner of an Organic Food Manufacturing Company and Health & Wellness Corporation

Number of Years in Current Position or Number of Years in the Position You're Most Known for Participating: Currently a business owner for over 20 years.

List the Previous Job Titles You've Had: Retirement Services Bank Intern, Trust Operations Bank Intern, Daycare Staffing Agency Office Manager, Restaurant Owner, Business Owner of an Organic Food & Beverage Manufacturing Company, Author of 20 Books, Professional Basketball Player in the United States and Overseas, Owner of Organic Food, Beverage & Vitamin Online Store, and Owner of a Health & Wellness Corporation.

List College Major(s), Master Degree(s), Doctoral Degree(s): Bachelor of Arts (BA) in English from the University of North Carolina at Charlotte.

1. **Who inspired you the most?** The inspiration that I used to encourage myself came from an aspect of my life that's much bigger than myself. I would go deep within myself to discover the goals closest to my heart to achieve my scholastic, athletic and career endeavors.

2. **What motivated you during the pursuit of your career?** My motivation stemmed from a desire to please my parents, family and myself. My parents sacrificed many things for my two older brothers and me. Their unselfish attitudes and contributions to our family gave me the passion I needed to be ready to take on anything that I encountered on the journey to my career.

3. **Who or what influenced you to achieve your goal(s) as a professional?** My family was the most influential proponents to the achievements that I strived to obtain. My father exhibited extremely hardworking qualities which complimented my mother's relentless passion to accomplish anything she set her mind to capture. They were two perfect examples of role models that I was fortunate enough to witness every day. I was, also, so privileged to have two older brothers who were my mentors as astute scholars and perennial leaders which provided guidance to me in all areas of my life. This paved the way for me into a successful journey as a student and athlete.

4. **What goal(s) did you set for yourself in attempting to reach your career aspiration(s)?** As a student, I committed myself to give my best effort in getting the best grades that I could to gain the knowledge I'd need to be the best I could in my future career in business. As an athlete, I always dreamed of playing professional basketball. I listened to those people who came before me. I was trained to learn as much as I could about the game of basketball while, at the same time, trying to perfect the fundamentals of basketball.

5. **What were your greatest strengths that you executed as a professional within your career?** It was and is important to be as consistent, diligent and hardworking as possible when I work every day. My greatest strengths evolved out observing my family and other people over the years who were successful. So, I followed in their footsteps and benefited, as well, from the same rewards resulting from the extra effort I put into being a person who perseveres.

6. **What most challenged you during your journey to becoming the professional in your occupation?** One of my biggest challenges as a professional was keeping up with the new innovations within the areas of business that I worked. I had to learn and adapt to the changes in technology and people's responses to those changes. These were consistent opportunities for me to seek out new methods to implement in meeting the needs of my customers and suppliers. I found that researching and studying regularly as a businessman was imperative in remaining relevant in the ever-evolving world of education, business, and sports.

7. **How did you manage your weaknesses within your occupation?** First, I had to be honest with myself to be able to identify my weaknesses. Once that was accomplished, I was able to see that in some cases I was behind the times on the new innovations and current technology. I asked others for assistance who were more advanced and familiar with those areas of business that I lacked. So, I researched those areas of my weaknesses to overcome my shortcomings. Sometimes it takes extra work and some extra time to

receive the knowledge needed to begin the process of improving on our weaknesses. Thus, it's important to be patient when you're trying to improve on your weaknesses as a student, athlete and professional within your career.

8. **How important was time management in performing well on your job?** Time Management was and still is very important in being as prepared and successful in whatever I plan to achieve. Time management has given me structure, order, and a schedule to execute my work more effectively. Learning this key component of success early on in my experiences as a student has enabled me to be better able to complete the business goals I set for myself.

9. **How much of your educational background factored into obtaining success in your field of work?** My educational background has been instrumental in providing the foundation to build off of to allow me to be productive in my career. Since I received an English degree in college, I was able to author many books, in addition to, studying and analyzing the strategies of basketball which enabled me to play professionally. Additionally, I received a certification in health & wellness nutrition which has afforded me the opportunity to assist people in improving their health. I've, also, been fortunate enough to operate businesses for the last twenty years. Therefore, as a student, study and try to retain as much knowledge as you can while learning the importance of the purposes of your acquired knowledge, and how it can apply to your field of study and future career.

10. What was your greatest accomplishment as a professional? As a professional, my greatest accomplishment occurred when I assisted my mother in overcoming a cancer that was thought to be "incurable". As a result of my involvement in helping to implement an organic food and vitamin program, my mother's health was successfully restored, consequently, destroying the cancer which saved her life. It was quite gratifying to receive confirmation of my mom's remission from this cancer as reported by her oncologist and other doctors. She was healed from this cancer without taking chemotherapy, radiation treatments, a stem-cell surgery or taking any medicines.

11. Why did you or do you work? Working is a necessity in life which fulfills my life. It's really enjoyable for me. I am fortunate to be able to work in areas of business which are passions of mine that I am extremely happy to be able to share with the world. My occupations are significant to me because they improve the quality of other people's lives.

12. What did you or do you value most about your occupation? I value the opportunity within running my businesses where I have the autonomy to decide what, how and when I can give resources and information to assist people in discovering, rededicating or encouraging my clients. It's important that we all should value the time we have in life and the opportunities to achieve the highest level of service we can for our families, our communities and ourselves.

13. **What advice would you give your 8th-grade self as a student preparing for a future career?** The message that I would focus on every day as an 8th-grade student centers on searching for the purpose in my life. I would identify what makes me passionate about life. I would look for the purpose in everything that I did, and ask myself why what I am doing is purposeful. Understanding the intent of a task, and how it is applied would be essential in determining why the intent was important. This would lead me to become more prepared for a career and life. As a student, I would have envisioned how my homework assignments could be applied to my life, family, goals, relationships, and dreams to attain the success that I desired. As an athlete, I'd make sure that as I trained, practiced and competed in competitions, I'd be mindful to always prepare mentally and physically with my purpose at the forefront of my thoughts.

14. **Last Word of Encouragement to the youth:** We don't become great by only doing the things we like, but greatness is achieved by committing ourselves to the needful and essential things of life that we don't like to do. Accordingly, our goals are met and positive change is achieved only when patterns of inconsistency are conquered.

15. **Do you have any future projects that I can promote for you to my readership audience?** Yes, the book that you're currently reading, right now, is my next project.

PRO SPORTS SPECIFIC JOBS

Aquatics & Program Director ~ Aquatics Director ~ Aquatics/Youth Coordinator ~ Area College Scout ~ Assistant Editor ~ Assistant Editor Social (Part-Time) ~ Assistant Golf Coach ~ Assistant Soccer Coach ~ Associate Aquatic Director ~ Associate Editor (NFL) ~ Association Aquatics Director ~ Athletic Team Coordinator ~ Baseball Assistant Head Coach ~ Baseball Business Development Coordinator ~ Baseball Instructor ~ Baseball Director ~ Baseball Head Coach ~ Baseball Operations Analyst ~ Baseball Publicist ~ Baseball R & D Developer ~ Baseball Sales Consultant ~ Baseball Specialist ~ Baseball Territory Specialist ~ Basketball Director ~ Basketball Operations Assistant ~ CEO of Sports Franchise ~ Client Partner Operations ~ Client Partner Security ~ Client Partner Vice President ~ Club/Team Service League Vice President ~ College Area Scout ~ Collegiate Baseball Placement Agent ~ Coordinator Basketball Operations ~ Coordinator for Student-Athlete Success ~ Coordinator Marketing Video Editor ~ Cycle Club Coordinator ~ Cycling Program Manager ~ Digital Sales Strategy Director ~ Digital Video Content Associate ~ Director of Aquatics & Wellness ~ Director of Golf ~ Director of Golf Operations ~ Director of Golf Sales ~ Director of Sales ~ Director of Soccer Operations ~ Director of Tennis ~ Director of Women's Basketball Operations ~ Director of Volleyball Operations ~ Event Services Coordinator ~ Female Hockey Coordinator ~ FIFA Assistant Content Producer ~ Football Director ~ Football Video Operations Manager ~ Global Merchandising Director ~ Global Partnerships National Sales Director ~ Global Partnerships Senior Manager ~ Global Senior Director Basketball ~ Global Strategy Director ~ Golf Assistant Head Coach ~ Golf Head Coach ~ Golfer Care Specialist ~ Golf Digital Merchandise Planner ~ Golf Sales Associate ~ Golf

Sales Manager ~ Golf Services Manager ~ Golf Shop Assistant ~ Golfer Support Agent ~ Golf Teaching Professional ~ Gymnastic Men's Assistant Head Coach ~ Gymnastic Men's Head Coach ~ Gymnastics Women's Assistant Head Coach ~ Gymnastics Women's Head Coach ~ Hockey Director ~ Hockey Sticks Senior Manager ~ Lacrosse Assistant Head Coach ~ Lacrosse Head Coach ~ Lacrosse Director ~ Lead Video Editor ~ Local Sports Coach ~ Marital Arts Instructor ~ Marketing Vice President ~ Men's & Women's Swim/Dive Assistant Coach ~ Men's Baseball Head Coach ~ Men's Basketball Assistant Coach ~ Men's Basketball Head Coach ~ Men's Field Hockey Assistant Coach ~ Men's Field Hockey Head Coach ~ Men's Ice Hockey Assistant Coach ~ Men's Ice Hockey Head Coach ~ Men's Soccer Assistant Coach ~ Men's Soccer Head Coach ~ Men's Volleyball Assistant Coach ~ Men's Volleyball Head Coach ~ Merchandising and Ecommerce Administrative Assistant ~ Multi-Platform Video Editor ~ NBA Insider ~ NBA Owner ~ NBA Senior Vice-President ~ NBA Talent Scout ~ NHL Social Media Community Manager ~ Partnership Marketing Director ~ Partnership Sales Director ~ Part-Time Soccer Coach ~ Part-Time Softball Instructor ~ Pro Baseball Apparel Digital Product Director ~ Pro Baseball Content Marketing Specialist ~ Pro Baseball Digital Content Associate ~ Pro Baseball Digital Content Coordinator ~ Pro Baseball Digital Co Pro Baseball Digital Marketplace Director ~ Content Producer ~ Pro Baseball Digital Content Specialist ~ Pro Baseball Digital Signage Technician ~ Pro Baseball DTC Capabilities Director ~ Pro Baseball Ecommerce Content Specialist ~ Pro Baseball Temporary Digital Content Producer ~ Pro Football Accounting Manager ~ Pro Football Accounts Payable Assistant ~ Pro Football Accounts Payable Purchaser ~ Pro Football Accounts Payable Specialist ~ Pro Football Administrative Assistant ~ Pro Football Administrative Assistant for Merchandise Operations ~ Pro Football Administration Coordinator ~ Pro Football Alumni Relations Manager ~ Pro Football Analytics & Football Research Coordinator ~ Pro Football Apparel

Merchandise Manager ~ Pro Football Apparel Assistant Merchandiser ~ Pro Football Apparel Digital Product Director ~ Pro Football Applications Developer ~ Pro Football Area Scout ~ Pro Football Assistant Athletic Trainer ~ Pro Football Assistant Athletic Trainer/Physical Therapist ~ Pro Football Assistant Director of Video ~ Pro Football Assistant Director of Video Operations ~ Pro Football Assistant Equipment Manager ~ Pro Football Assistant Groundskeeper ~ Pro Football Assistant Head Coach ~ Pro Football Assistant Manager of Safety and Event Security ~ Pro Football Assistant Merchandising Manager of Novelties and Stadium ~ Pro Football Assistant Offensive Line Coach ~ Pro Football Assistant Warehouse Manager ~ Pro Football Audio/Video Manager ~ Pro Football Audio/Video Technician ~ Pro Football Business Administration ~ Pro Football Business & Football Systems Manager ~ Pro Football Business Analytics Coordinator ~ Pro Football Business Development Coordinator ~ Pro Football Cheerleader Director ~ Pro Football Cheerleader Head Coach ~ Pro Football Chief Financial Officer ~ Pro Football Content Marketing Specialist ~ Pro Football Creative Development ~ Pro Football Business Analytics Manager ~ Pro Football Chairman ~ Pro Football Club Events Manager ~ Pro Football Coaching Assistant ~ Pro Football College Scout ~ Pro Football College/Pro Scout ~ Pro Football College Scouting Coordinator ~ Pro Football College Scouting Senior Assistant ~ Pro Football Community Relations Administrative Assistant ~ Pro Football Community Relations Manager ~ Pro Football Conditioning Assistant ~ Pro Football Conditioning Coordinator ~ Pro Football Controller ~ Pro Football Conversion and Cleaning Supervisor ~ Pro Football Corporate Communications Manager ~ Pro Football Corporate Partnerships Client Services Coordinator ~ Pro Football Corporate Partnerships Manager ~ Pro Football Courier ~ Pro Football Creative Services Manager ~ Pro Football Creative Services and Brand Manager ~ Pro Football Defensive Backs Coach ~ Pro Football Defensive Coordinator ~ Pro Football Defensive Line Coach ~ Pro Football Desktop Support Analyst ~ Pro

Football Digital Commerce Production Coordinator ~ Pro Football Digital Commerce Site Marketing & Merchandise Manager ~ Pro Football Digital Commerce Visual Designer ~ Pro Football Digital Content Associate ~ Pro Football Digital Content Coordinator ~ Pro Football Digital Content Producer ~ Pro Football Digital Content Specialist ~ Pro Football Digital Marketplace Director ~ Pro Football Digital Media Coordinator ~ Pro Football Digital Media Manager ~ Pro Football Digital Signage Technician ~ Pro Football DTC Capabilities Director ~ Pro Football Director of Club Events & Operations ~ Pro Football Director of Communications ~ Pro Football Director of Content ~ Pro Football Director of Corporate Partnerships & Activation ~ Pro Football Director of Ecommerce ~ Pro Football Director of Events ~ Pro Football Director of Facilities ~ Pro Football Director of Fan Experience ~ Pro Football Director of Financial Planning and Analysis ~ Pro Football Director of Football Administration ~ Pro Football Director of Foundation and Civic Affairs ~ Pro Football Director of General Merchandise Manager ~ Pro Football Director of Marketing & Events ~ Pro Football Director of Merchandise Operations ~ Pro Football Director of Player Personnel ~ Pro Football Director of Production ~ Pro Football Director of Service & Activation ~ Pro Football Director of Stadium Event Operations ~ Pro Football Director of Stadium Security ~ Pro Football Director of Suite Sales ~ Pro Football Director of Stadium Event Operations ~ Pro Football Director of Team Fans ~ Pro Football Director of Team Fans Community Management Specialist ~ Pro Football Director of Team Fans Marketing Coordinator ~ Pro Football Director of Team Fans Program Manager ~ Pro Football Director of Team Security ~ Pro Football Director of Ticketing ~ Pro Football Director of Ticket Operations ~ Pro Football Director of Video & Facilities ~ Pro Football Director of Video Operations ~ Pro Football Ecommerce Content Specialist ~ Pro Football Electrician ~ Pro Football Email Marketing Manager ~ Pro Football Email Specialist ~ Pro Football Equipment Director ~ Pro Football Equipment/Field Assistant ~ Pro Football Equipment

Manager ~ Pro Football Event Coordinator ~ Pro Football Event Marketing Manager ~ Pro Football Events Manager ~ Pro Football Event Operations ~ Pro Football Event Sales Manager ~ Pro Football Event Services Administrator ~ Pro Football Event Services Manager ~ Pro Football Executive Administrative Assistant ~ Pro Football Executive Assistant to the CFO ~ Pro Football Executive Assistant to the President ~ Pro Football Executive Producer ~ Pro Football Executive Vice-President of Business Operations ~ Pro Football Field Manager/Assistant Equipment Manager ~ Pro Football Facilities Manager ~ Pro Football Fan Communications and Loyalty Coordinator ~ Pro Football Fan Experience Manager ~ Pro Football Fan Experience Representative ~ Pro Football Financial Analyst ~ Pro Football Fulfillment and Logistics Manager ~ Pro Football Game Day Producer ~ Pro Football General Manager ~ Pro Football Grounds Keeping Staff ~ Pro Football Group Sales Account Executive ~ Pro Football Group Sales Manager ~ Pro Football Group Sales Representative ~ Pro Football Group Sales Senior Account Executive ~ Pro Football Head Athletic Trainer ~ Pro Football Head Coach ~ Pro Football Head Groundskeeper ~ Pro Football Human Resources Manager ~ Pro Football HVAC Technician ~ Pro Football Inside Linebacker Coach ~ Pro Football Internal Medicine Physician ~ Pro Football IT Service Desk Technician ~ Pro Football Landscape & Field Maintenance ~ Pro Football Lead Web Developer ~ Pro Football Luxury Suite Manager ~ Pro Football Mascot Coordinator ~ Pro Football Manager of Game and Event Entertainment ~ Pro Football Manager of Guest Experience & Tours ~ Pro Football Manager of Production ~ Pro Football Manager of Replenishment ~ Pro Football Manager of Safety and Event Security ~ Pro Football Manager of Ticket Sales ~ Pro Football Manager of Youth Outreach ~ Pro Football Marketing and Foundation Coordinator ~ Pro Football Marketing Coordinator ~ Pro Football Media Production Specialist ~ Pro Football Merchandise Accounting Manager ~ Pro Football Merchandising Manager of Novelties and Stadium ~ Pro

Football Merchandise Planning Manager ~ Pro Football Network & Security Engineer ~ Pro Football Network & Security Manager ~ Pro Football Network Architect ~ Pro Football Neurosurgery Physician ~ Pro Football Offensive Coordinator ~ Pro Football Offensive Line Coach ~ Pro Football Operations Coordinator ~ Pro Football Operations Manager ~ Pro Football Operations Staff ~ Pro Football Orthopedic Surgery Physician ~ Pro Football Outside Linebackers Coach ~ Pro Football Partnership Activation Manager ~ Pro Football Partnership Administrator ~ Pro Football Partnership Coordinator ~ Pro Football Partnership Activation Specialist ~ Pro Football Payroll/Benefits Coordinator ~ Pro Football Payroll/Accounting Coordinator ~ Pro Football Payroll Manager ~ Pro Football Personnel Executive ~ Pro Football Player Engagement Coordinator ~ Pro Football Player Engagement Director ~ Pro Football Player Personnel Assistant ~ Pro Football Player Personnel Coordinator ~ Pro Football Playing Surface Staff ~ Pro Football Plumber ~ Pro Football Premium Seating Account Executive ~ Pro Football Premium Seating Sales Manager ~ Pro Football Project Coordinator ~ Pro Football Project Cost Coordinator ~ Pro Football President ~ Pro Football Public Relations Assistant ~ Pro Football Public Relations/Media Manager ~ Pro Football Quarterback Coach ~ Pro Football Receptionist ~ Pro Football Running Backs Coach ~ Pro Football Salary Cap and Legal Executive ~ Pro Football Scouting Coordinator ~ Pro Football Season Ticket Assistant ~ Pro Football Security Officer ~ Pro Football Security Supervisor ~ Pro Football Senior Accountant/Analyst ~ Pro Football Senior Project Manager ~ Pro Football Senior Vice President of Business Operations ~ Pro Football Shipping and Receiving Manager ~ Pro Football Skilled Maintenance ~ Pro Football Social Media Director ~ Pro Football Special Projects ~ Pro Football Special Team Coordinator ~ Pro Football Sports Turf Operations Manager ~ Pro Football Stadium Accounting Manager ~ Pro Football Stadium Event Operations Manager ~ Pro Football Stadium Operations Administrative Assistant ~ Pro Football Stadium Operations

Receptionist ~ Pro Football Stadium Payroll Coordinator ~ Pro Football Stadium Services Coordinator ~ Pro Football Stadium Services Manager ~ Pro Football Stadium Services Supervisor ~ Pro Football Staff Accountant ~ Pro Football Stationary Engineer ~ Pro Football Store Operations & Special Projects Division Manager ~ Pro Football Suite Services Coordinator ~ Pro Football Suite Sales Manager ~ Pro Football Support Liaison ~ Pro Football Systems Administrator ~ Pro Football Systems Engineer ~ Pro Football Team Assistant Magazine Editor ~ Pro Football Team Authentic & Memorabilia Manager ~ Pro Football Team Magazine Editor ~ Pro Football Team Photographer ~ Pro Football Team Security Supervisor ~ Pro Football Technology Director ~ Pro Football Temporary Digital Content Producer ~ Pro Football Ticket Office Coordinator ~ Pro Football Ticket Office Manager ~ Pro Football Ticket Office Services Specialist ~ Pro Football Ticket Operations Assistant ~ Pro Football Ticket Sales & Retention ~ Pro Football Ticket Sales Representative ~ Pro Football Tight Ends Coach ~ Pro Football TV Team Reporter ~ Pro Football Wide Receivers Coach ~ Pro Football Utility Maintenance ~ Pro Football Vice-President ~ Pro Football Vice President of Administration ~ Pro Football Vice President of Corporate Partnership & Premium Sales ~ Pro Football Vice-President of Finance ~ Pro Football Vice-President of Football & Business Administration ~ Pro Football Vice-President of Planning & Development ~ Pro Football Vice President of Stadium Operations & Management ~ Pro Football Vice-President of Technology ~ Pro Football Vice-President Sales & Marketing ~ Pro Football Vice-President of Sports Medicine and Performance ~ Pro Football Vice President of Stadium Services and Events ~ Pro Football Video Assistant ~ Pro Football Video Producer ~ Pro Football Video Production Manager ~ Pro Football Warehouse and Designated Categories Allocation Manager ~ Pro Football Warehouse Manager ~ Pro Football Youth and High School Football Marketing Manager ~ Pro Sports Accountant Assistant ~ Pro Sports Administration Assistant ~ Pro Sports

Assistant Men's Golf Coach ~ Pro Sports Assistant Superintendent ~ Pro Sports Assistant Women's Basketball Coach ~ Pro Sports Assistant Women's Basketball Coach ~ Pro Sports Assistant Women's Lacrosse Coach ~ Pro Sports Assistant Women's Soccer Coach ~ Pro Sports Club President ~ Pro Sports Clubhouse Assistant ~ Pro Sports Group Sales Executive ~ Pro Sports Human Resources Vice President ~ Pro Sports Men's Golf Head Coach ~ Pro Sports Mid-Level Designer/Animator ~ Pro Sports Part-Time Inside Sales Representative ~ Pro Sports Product Vice President ~ Pro Sports Production Assistant ~ Pro Sports Retail Divisional Vice President ~ Pro Sports Sales Manager ~ Pro Sports Senior Payroll Administrator ~ Pro Sports Sponsorship Services Coordinator ~ Pro Sports Sponsorship Team President ~ Pro Sports Sponsorship Team Vice President ~ Pro Sports Talent Acquisition Vice President ~ Pro Sports Technology Vice President ~ Pro Sports Ticket Sales Team Vice President ~ Pro Sports Vice President of Operations ~ Pro Sports Video Operations Assistant Manager ~ Pro Sports Women's Basketball Head Coach ~ Pro Sports Women's Lacrosse Head Coach ~ Pro Sports Women's Soccer Coach ~ Pro Track Head Coach ~ Reporter and Football Beat Writer ~ Resident Camp Program Director ~ Senior Aquatics Director ~ Senior Deputy Editor ~ Senior Video Editor ~ Soccer Director ~ Soccer Men's Assistant Head Coach ~ Soccer Men's Head Coach ~ Soccer Women's Assistant Head Coach ~ Soccer Women's Head Coach ~ Soccer Sports Data Specialist ~ Social Programmer Temp (NBA) ~ Social Video Producer/Editor ~ Softball Assistant Head Coach ~ Softball Head Coach ~ Softball Territory Specialist ~ Sports Agent ~ Sports Broadcaster ~ Swim Assistant Head Coach ~ Swim Head Coach ~ Swim Instructor ~ Swim Lesson Instructor ~ Swim Supervisor ~ Talent Buyer Vice President ~ Team Chaplain ~ Tennis Assistant Head Coach ~ Tennis Associate ~ Tennis Coordinator ~ Tennis Head Coach ~ Tennis Head Coach (Men's) ~ Tennis Head Coach (Women's) ~ Track and Field Footwear Product Line Manager ~ Traveling Swim Instructor ~ Triathlon Assistant Head Coach ~ Triathlon Head

Coach ~ UFC Rendering Engineer ~ Venue Community Support Manager ~ Vice President of Event Sales ~ Vice President of Finance ~ Vice President of Operations ~ Vice President of Sales ~ Video Editor ~ Volleyball Assistant Coach ~ Volleyball Head Coach ~ Web Based Editor (Part-Time) ~ Women's Basketball Assistant Coach ~ Women's Basketball Director Player Development ~ Women's Basketball Head Coach ~ Women's Field Hockey Assistant Coach ~ Women's Field Hockey Head Coach ~ Women's Ice Hockey Assistant Coach ~ Women's Ice Hockey Head Coach ~ Women's Lacrosse Assistant Media Relations ~ Women's Lacrosse Head Coach ~ Women's Soccer Assistant Coach ~ Women's Soccer Head Coach ~ Women's Swimming Assistant Coach ~ Women's Swimming Head Coach Youth & Street Community Hockey Coordinator ~ Wrestling Assistant Head Coach ~ Wrestling Head Coach ~ Youth Dance Instructor ~ Youth Soccer Assistant Head Coach ~ Youth Soccer Camp Coach ~ Youth Soccer Head Coach ~ Youth Soccer Instructor ~ Youth Soccer Instructor/Coach ~ Youth Sports Director ~ Youth Training Programs Coach.

SPORTS PROFESSIONAL PROFILE
ALL STUDENTS, AND PARTICULARLY, STUDENT-ATHLETES, "DO YOU HAVE A PLAN B?

Professional Occupation Questionnaire for Student Academic & Career Developmental Exposure

Name: Tunch Ilkin

Your Current Job Title and/or the Job You're Most Known for Participating: NFL Player for 14 years (1st Player to Play in the NFL from Turkey)

Number of Years in Current Position or Number of Years in the Position You're Most Known for Participating: NFL Offensive Lineman for (13 years with the Pittsburgh Steelers & 1 year with Green Bay Packers) totaling 14 years

List the Previous Job Titles You've Had: Delivered Newspapers, Caddy, Coach & Umpire for Little League Baseball, Shoveling Scrap Iron (hardest job I ever had), Day Camp Counselor, Construction Worker (Mixed Mortar & Carried Bricks), Carpenter, Pizza Restaurant Employee, Health Club Employee, NFL Player, TV & Radio Broadcaster, Men's Ministry Pastor.

List College Major(s), Master Degree(s), Doctoral Degree(s): Indiana State University, Broadcasting Degree

1. **Who inspired you the most?** Mike Webster, John Kolb, and Larry Brown were my Pittsburgh Steeler teammates who I observed of their hard work, diligence, and commitment to being the best players at their positions. I saw them coming in early to practice to lift weights and watch film consistently, as I would

walk through the building, which led me to do those same things. During my senior year of high school, my head coach was a great motivator, who definitely inspired me. He said that he believed I could play in college, and that encouraged me to work toward that goal. My offensive line coach said that if I worked hard, then I could make it to the professional level.

2. **What motivated you during the pursuit of your career?** I wanted to be the best that I could as a player in the game of football. During the 1983 NFL season, I had a terrible game against the all-pro defensive end, Lyle Alzado. After that poor performance, I began working with a martial artist to improve the skills needed for using my hands more effectively. As a result of seeking out extra assistance to enhance my craft as an offensive lineman during my playing days, I received opportunities to coach after I retired as a football player. Some NFL coaches observed the techniques I had developed while I played for the Steelers after receiving martial arts training, and they offered me the platform to teach my techniques after I retired from playing. The NFL coaches watched videos of my previous games and came up with the name, "Tunch Punch", for the technique I used as an offensive lineman to create an advantage against my opponent. The exposure from these training opportunities led to me being asked to teach other NFL teams my techniques. This was the driving force to me being offered multiple NFL coaching job positions. Additionally, I was privileged enough to speak at many football conferences and team practices which further exposed my football skills to many other

football professionals, and ultimately the next generation of NFL players. I was offered many NFL coaching opportunities over the years, but I decided to embark on a television and radio broadcasting career covering football.

3. **Who or what influenced you to achieve your goal(s) as a professional?** My dad influenced me the most because he had the courage to bring us, here, to America from Turkey. He worked extremely hard to provide for my family, and this gave me the example in life I needed to pattern my work ethic after him.

4. **What goal(s) did you set for yourself in attempting to reach your career aspiration(s)?** I really didn't set too many goals for myself, even though, I wanted to play football in college and the NFL. Fortunately, I worked hard and was committed to giving my best effort which produced a professional football career.

5. **What were your greatest strengths that you executed as a professional within your career?** This is a hard question for me to answer because I really don't feel comfortable with telling of the strengths that I possess. I look at my strengths as a gift. My greatest strength, physically, I guess would be seen in my hands as an offensive lineman moving my opponent. I believed in working hard, in which, produced internal strength within me. Other strengths that could be seen in me were ones that other people selected me to positions such as team captain and player personnel team representative. If people looked at me as an athlete, they probably would not have thought that I

played in the NFL. However, I was able to work hard enough to achieve what I did as a professional football player.

6. **What most challenged you during your journey to becoming the professional in your occupation?** The overwhelming task of competing against bigger athletes was my biggest challenge. I was undersized for my position, and I had to be really in-tune with my techniques to excel against my bigger opponents. The techniques I used put added pressure on my joints which presented me with other health issues I had to manage during my playing days. Developing confidence was another challenge I faced early on in my NFL career. I came from a smaller college, so, the level of talent was much greater in the NFL, and I had to get used to that and raise my level of play. I, also, had to learn how to manage my nervousness every time I played a game. I was nervous before every game that I played because I didn't want to let my teammates down. I always had a fear of failure that never left me. My teammate, Mike Webster, used to say, "Fear is a great motivator" which became true in my case to produce better results on the field. When fear was there in my career, it caused me to prepare harder, work harder and it caused me to never leave anything to chance. Fear became a driving force to motivate me throughout my career to achieve more.

7. **How did you manage your weaknesses within your occupation?** When I watched the videotapes of my games, I was able to study the films of my games which showed my mistakes. My film study gave me the opportunity to see and realize my mistakes and use

other techniques in practice for the purpose of incorporating these new skills in the games. As a result, the games were often times easier, because I was practicing these new techniques against some of the greatest defensive players in the game.

8. **How important was time management in performing well on your job?** Time management was essential to maintaining a high level of preparation, skill, and motivation, in order, for me to place myself in a position to give my best effort. For example, I was obsessed so much with working out that I would make sure that my vacation plans included places that had a gym for me to use, as I did even on my honeymoon. Preparation is something I learned while I played. Now, that I am retired, I devote time, also, to prepare for radio and television segments as I commentate or the study time I need to prepare as a pastor. So, using your time wisely as you prepare for life's tasks is essential in producing good results. My Pittsburgh Steeler former head coach, Chuck Noll, used to say, "Football is temporary, you have to get ready for your life's work", and this is so important for seeing life in the proper perspective.

9. **How much of your educational background factored into obtaining success in your field of work?** I was not a serious student in college or high school, but I became a student of football later on in life which helped when I was studying to be a pastor.

10. What was your greatest accomplishment as a professional? I don't think of my accomplishments as what I achieved, but I think of my accomplishments as more of receiving gifts. As an NFL player, I view the accomplishment of making a Pro Bowl as a gift, and not as my own doing. I, also, love being a dad and grandfather.

11. Why did you or do you work? First, I work to make a living. I'm fortunate enough to work because I get a chance to teach football, and I counsel people regarding life's issues to help enrich their lives.

12. What did you or do you value most about your occupation? During my career, what I valued most was to appreciate the gift I was given to become a professional athlete which led me to be able to help more people.

13. What advice would you give your 8th-grade self as a student preparing for a future career? Get serious about learning. I wish I was a serious student back when I was in school. Pittsburgh Steeler former head coach Chuck Noll used to say, "You are either getting better or worse." It's important to use every opportunity to get better. I believe that we should use every day to grow.

14. Last Word of Encouragement to the youth: Help one another, and this is the mindset the youth should have toward one another on the field and in life. It is important for our young kids and young adults to be great teammates, mentors, and encouragers to each other. As an athlete, the best effort you can give is to be a great teammate.

15. Do you have any future projects that I can promote for you to my readership audience? Tunch & Wolf - Light of Life Walk (annual event)

STUDENT AND STUDENT-ATHLETE PLAN B BOOK
ALL STUDENTS, AND PARTICULARLY, STUDENT-ATHLETES, "DO YOU HAVE A PLAN B?

Professional Occupation Questionnaire for Student Academic & Career Developmental Exposure

Name: Kelvin Torve

Your Current Job Title and/or the Job You're Most Known for Participating: Head Coach of a 19 and under Baseball Team – American Legion Baseball Post 22 Hardhats of Rapid City, South Dakota.

Number of Years in Current Position or Number of Years in the Position You're Most Known for Participating: Currently a Head Coach in his first year for a 19 and under baseball league, Major League Professional Baseball Player for 3 years and 2-year baseball player in Japanese Professional League.

List the Previous Job Titles You've Had: Major League Baseball Player, Sales, and Development Director at a Classical Christian School.

List College Major(s), Master Degree(s), Doctoral Degree(s): Bachelor of Science of (BS) in Marketing, Oral Roberts University.

1. **Who inspired you the most?** A number of professional athletes inspired me most.

2. **What motivated you during the pursuit of your career?** My motivation during the pursuit of my career existed, because of my passion to work and desire to provide for my family.

3. **Who or what influenced you to achieve your goal(s) as a professional?** My family was the most influencing component of my life motivating me toward achieving my goals.

4. **What goal(s) did you set for yourself in attempting to reach your career aspiration(s)?** I sought after a career in which I was passionate. I looked at an occupation, not as a job, but rather, a passion.

5. **What were your greatest strengths that you executed as a professional within your career?** My greatest strengths consisted of being a person of diligence and perseverance.

6. **What most challenged you during your journey to becoming the professional in your occupation?** Procrastination and lack of passion in previous employment opportunities are what challenged me most along my journey.

7. **How did you manage your weaknesses within your occupation?** I managed them by recognizing them as weaknesses, and I had to be diligent in trying to overcome them.

8. **How important was time management in performing well on your job?** Time Management was very important, as I was in charge of my own schedule. If I didn't pay attention to time management, then it would have gotten away from me.

9. **How much of your educational background factored into obtaining success in your field of work?** In my profession, education was not as much of a factor as other factors.

10. **What was your greatest accomplishment as a professional?** Playing in the Major Leagues was my greatest accomplishment.

11. **Why did you or do you work?** I work to provide for my family, and to speak into other peoples' lives.

12. **What did you or do you value most about your occupation?** I value the relationships with people the most.

13. **What advice would you give your 8th-grade self as a student preparing for a future career?** It is important to discover your passion!

SOCIAL MEDIA JOBS

Athletics Multi Media Assistant ~ Athletics Social Media Director ~ Board Operator ~ Content/Vice President ~ Content/Social Media Manager ~ Finance Vice President ~ Global Product Vice President ~ Global Strategy Vice President ~ Graphics Playback Operator ~ Group Sales Account Executive ~ Inside Sales Consultant ~ Inside Sales Executive ~ National Sales Vice President ~ Marketing Vice President ~ Media Board Operator ~ Media Programming Professional ~ Media Rights Consulting Analyst ~ Part-Time Board Operator ~ Pro Football Senior Social Media Editor ~ Pro Football Social Media Coordinator ~ Pro Football Social Media Director ~ Pro Football Media Manager ~ Pro Football Social Media Marketing Associate ~ Retail Divisional Vice President ~ Retail Sales Associate ~ Retail Sales Specialist ~ Sales Associate ~ Sales Lead ~ Sales Representative ~ Screen Print Hand Print Operator ~ Senior Social Media Coordinator ~ Social Marketing Specialist ~ Social Media & Video Coordinator ~ Social Media Coordinator ~ Social Media Director ~ Social Media Graphics Producer ~ Social Media Marketing Associate ~ Social Media Manager ~ Social Media Preditor ~ Social Media Production Assistant ~ Social Media Senior Program Manager ~ Sports Media Sales Professional ~ Studio Operator ~ Talent Acquisition Vice President ~ Ticker Operator ~ Trackman Operator ~ Video Board Operator.

STUDENT AND STUDENT-ATHLETE PLAN B BOOK

ALL STUDENTS, AND PARTICULARLY, STUDENT-ATHLETES,

"DO YOU HAVE A <u>PLAN B</u>?

Professional Occupation Profile for Student Academic & Career Developmental Exposure

CORPORATE PROFILE – Make-A-Wish America Foundation

MISSION STATEMENT
Together, we create life-changing wishes for children with critical illnesses.

MAKE-A-WISH PHENOMENON REACHES FAR & WIDE
Make-A-Wish® is the nation's largest wish-granting organization. It has fulfilled the wishes of **more than 300,000 children** in the United States and its territories since 1980. Headquartered in Phoenix, Make-A-Wish serves every community in the United States, Guam, and Puerto Rico through its 62 chapters.

WHY WISHES MATTER
Research shows children who have wishes granted build the physical and emotional strength needed to fight a critical illness. This may **improve their quality of life** and **produce better health outcomes.**

BEGINNINGS OF MAKE-A-WISH

In 1980, Chris Greicius, a 7-year-old boy diagnosed with leukemia, wanted nothing more than to become a police officer. Law enforcement officers heard about Chris' wish to be a police officer and responded to the call. A police helicopter flew him to Arizona Department of Public Safety headquarters for a tour. Chris experienced the thrill of riding in a patrol car and was named the first-ever honorary state patrolman in Arizona history. The law enforcement community also presented him a custom-tailored uniform, motorcycle helmet, campaign hat and the motorcycle wings he earned on his own battery-powered bike. Many of those responsible for fulfilling Chris' wish wanted to do the same for other children with life-threatening medical conditions and founded the Make-A-Wish Foundation® in November 1980.

WHO IS ELIGIBLE?

We grant the wishes of medically eligible children who:
- have been diagnosed with a progressive, degenerative or malignant condition that has placed the child's life in jeopardy;
- are older than 2½ and younger than 18 (at the time of referral);
- have not received a wish from another wish-granting organization.

The child's physician, certified nurse practitioner or certified physician assistant determines whether a child is medically eligible to receive a wish. An important clarification is that *wish kids are not necessarily terminal*. The misconception exists because it was true for a few years immediately after the organization's founding. However, the eligibility criteria expanded many years ago to allow doctors to use the wish as an important part of the medical treatment and healing process.

CORPORATE PROFILE – Make-A-Wish America Foundation

FUNDING SOURCES
Make-A-Wish is a 501(c)(3) tax-exempt organization that relies on the generous contributions of **individuals, corporate sponsorships, planned gifts,** and **grants** to make life-changing wishes possible. Make-A-Wish **does not** raise funds by door-to-door, telephone solicitation methods or receive funding from federal, state or local government programs. In-kind donations of goods and services such as frequent flier miles and hotel loyalty points also help finance our mission. Seventy-four percent of expenses nationwide are devoted to the mission – far exceeding the program service allocation standards set forth by the nation's leading charity watchdog groups, including the Council of Better Business Bureaus' Wise Giving Alliance.

VOLUNTEERING
More than 35,000 volunteers generously give their time and energy to fulfill the Make-A-Wish mission. Volunteers serve Make-A-Wish chapters across the country in a variety of capacities including wish granting, office administrative support, language translation, special event planning and coordinating, website design, fundraising and much more. People can offer to volunteer through the "Ways to Help" section of the national website, wish.org, or by contacting their local Make-A-Wish chapter.

KIDS FOR WISH KIDS®: A number of Make-A-Wish chapters across the country coordinate a Kids For Wish Kids program, which enables children to raise money in their schools to help grant wishes. Kids For Wish Kids is unique because kids manage it themselves. Although each chapter does not have a Kids For Wish Kids program, there are opportunities in every Make-A-Wish community for young people to help make wishes come true.

SPORTS-RELATED JOB ROLES

There are a couple of departments within the Make-A-Wish Foundation which support athletic operations within the organization. The first department is the Entertainment and Sports Team which support the relationships with athletes.

Managers and **coordinators** work together to manage this area of service. The Wish Department is the second department which provides **manager** and **coordinator positions** at most of the 62 Make-A-Wish chapters nationwide to carry out wish requests at the local level, including wishes for athletes on local sports teams.

THE WISH PROCESS

Currently, Make-A-Wish grants more than **15,000 wishes** for children with critical illnesses in the U.S. every year, but there remains a tremendous gap between the number of wishes we grant today and the estimated **27,000 children** in the United States that are diagnosed with a qualifying condition annually.

Every wish has the ability to help wish families replace fear with confidence, sadness with joy and anxiety with hope. Make-A-Wish follows a process to create life-changing wish experiences for each wish kid.

STEP ONE: The Wish Referral
Out of respect for the privacy of the children and families Make-A-Wish serves, only these sources may refer a child:
- a medical professional treating the child (doctor, nurse, social worker or child-life specialist);
- the child's parents or legal guardians;
- the potential wish child.

CORPORATE PROFILE – Make-A-Wish America Foundation

STEP TWO: Determining the Child's Eligibility
Children older than 2½ and younger than 18 (at the time of referral) who are diagnosed with a life-threatening medical condition may be eligible for a wish. The treating physician, certified nurse practitioner or certified physician assistant determines whether a child is medically eligible to receive a wish. A child also must not have received a wish from another wish-granting organization to qualify. There are no other qualifications based on sex, race, religion, socioeconomic status or any other demographic category.

STEP THREE: Choosing a Wish
Once the child is deemed medically eligible, we send one of our enthusiastic wish teams to learn the child's one true wish. These passionate volunteers help children explore their imaginations for the experience that will forever change them for the better.

Wishes generally fall into one of these categories:

I wish to have...
I wish to be...
I wish to go...
I wish to meet...
I wish to give...

STEP FOUR: Making a Wish Come True
Finally, our wish granters create an unforgettable experience driven by the wish kid's creativity. The experience makes lives better for the children, their families and sometimes their entire community. All members of the wish kid's immediate family take part in the wish whenever possible, and all wish expenses are fully covered by Make-A-Wish – giving the wish kid and family a respite from the stress of dealing with a critical illness.

In many cases, the allure of a wish experience is a source of inspiration for children undergoing difficult medical treatments and a positive force that helps them overcome their obstacles.

WISHES BY THE NUMBERS

Since its founding in 1980, Make-A-Wish has granted **more than 300,000 wishes**. Today, we grant a wish **every 34 minutes**. Much like their imaginations, children's wishes cover an almost limitless spectrum. From wishing to be a ballerina to meeting a favorite celebrity; from receiving a new laptop computer to visiting a glamorous destination, wish children have enjoyed unforgettable, inspirational wish experiences around the world.

In the fiscal year 2017, Make-A-Wish granted more than **15,400 wishes**, the most ever in its 38-year history. The most popular wish is to visit a theme park, which accounts for more than 40 percent of the requests from our wish kids.

The average cost of a wish nationwide in FY2017 was **$10,682**, which includes cash and in-kind support.

CORPORATE PROFILE – Make-A-Wish America Foundation

CHARITY RATINGS AND BRAND ACCOLADES
- Make-A-Wish holds the **Better Business Bureaus' Wise Giving Alliance Seal**, becoming one of the first charities to earn the designation.

- According to the 2018 Harris Poll EquiTrend®, Make-A-Wish is:
    - One of the top 7 brands in the health nonprofit category
    - Ranked in the top 25% for brand equity among all for-profit and nonprofit brands
    - Ranked in the top 10% for all U.S. brands for trust, social impact, shared values, and reputation.

ABOUT MAKE-A-WISH
Make-A-Wish creates life-changing wishes for children with critical illnesses. We seek to bring every eligible child's wish to life because a wish is an integral part of a child's treatment journey. Research shows children who have wishes granted can build the physical and emotional strength they need to fight their illness. Headquartered in Phoenix, Arizona, Make-A-Wish is the world's leading children's wish-granting organization, serving children in every community in the United States and in more than 50 countries worldwide. Together, generous donors, supporters, staff and more than 35,000 volunteers across the U.S., grant a wish every 34 minutes, on average, somewhere in the country. Since 1980, Make-A-Wish has granted more than 300,000 wishes to children in the U.S. and its territories; more than 15,400 in 2017 alone. For more information about Make-A-Wish America, visit wish.org.

STUDENT AND STUDENT-ATHLETE PLAN B BOOK
ALL STUDENTS, AND PARTICULARLY, STUDENT-ATHLETES, "DO YOU HAVE A PLAN B?

Professional Occupation Questionnaire for Student Academic & Career Developmental Exposure

Name: Shaina Reeser

Your Current Job Title and/or the Job You're Most Known for Participating: Director of Entertainment & Sports Relations at Make-A-Wish America

Number of Years in Current Position or Number of Years in the Position You're Most Known for Participating: I've spent 11 years at Make-A-Wish, starting as a celebrity project coordinator. My focus was on sports for many years as the sports relations manager, and I later was promoted to a senior manager in the department. I am currently the Director of Entertainment & Sports Relations. My role is to oversee the team responsible for fostering and developing our relationships with celebrities, including entertainers, musicians, actors, online influencers and athletes. Celebrities are an integral part of the Make-A-Wish community fulfilling more than 1,000 wishes a year for kids who wish to meet them. In addition, athletes, and other celebrities can be incredibly impactful from a fundraising standpoint either by personally donating or by enlisting their network of fans and other influencers to raise funds or drive awareness for Make-A-Wish.

List the Previous Job Titles You've Had: I started my career as a part-time receptionist for a minor league hockey team where I answered phones, registered kids for youth hockey teams and even wore the mascot costume one night when a colleague called in sick. While pursuing my degree, I worked as a student assistant in the recruiting department for a Big Ten football team and led a team of 30 students who helped host recruiting visits to campus. Later, I went to the National Basketball Association where I worked for the Indiana Pacers in community relations and Phoenix Suns in new business development.

List College Major(s), Master Degree(s), Doctoral Degree(s): Bachelor of Arts (B.A) in Political Science from Purdue University with a minor in communications and women's studies

1. **Who inspired you the most?** My parents supported my career goals and taught me the value of hard work.

2. **What motivated you during the pursuit of your career?** I am naturally competitive and love learning. So, both of these qualities have kept me intrinsically motivated at work.

3. **Who or what influenced you to achieve your goal(s) as a professional?** My first job with a minor league hockey team showed me how a team can connect to their community and this inspired me to pursue a career in sports.

4. **What goal(s) did you set for yourself in attempting to reach your career aspiration(s)?** My goal is to achieve success and stay balanced. Being naturally competitive, I often need a reminder to pace myself. As a working mom with two small kids, it is important for me to be flexible with goals and timelines.

5. **What were your greatest strengths that you executed as a professional within your career?** I've been consistent and available to help with any challenge facing the team

6. **What most challenged you during your journey to becoming the professional in your occupation?** As an introvert, my time in new business development with the Phoenix Suns was extremely challenging. It took me out of my comfort zone and required me to build rapport with clients quickly and efficiently. That job also built my confidence when I was able to overcome my natural shyness.

7. **How did you manage your weaknesses within your occupation?** My team granted around 1,200 wishes involving the entertainment and sports community last year. Since wishes don't just happen on their own, Make-A-Wish is only able to create life-changing wish experiences with help from others. As a result, my team does everything we can to build strong relationships with celebrities and provide best-in-class customer service. We also must be able to adapt quickly and think creatively in order to keep up with the constantly changing list of sports, music, fashion, film and YouTube icons who kids wish to meet. We

rely on collaboration and support of those who champion our mission in the industry to help us grant wishes.

8. **How important was time management in performing well on your job?** Responsiveness is the most critical element of time management in my current job. My team works with celebrities and athletes who have very busy schedules. We also work with Make-A-Wish families who are balancing a never-ending rotation of doctor's appointments on top of school, work and their busy family lives. Time is often the biggest challenge in bringing everyone together to grant a child's wish. Timely responses and ongoing communication are key to making wishes happen.

9. **How much of your educational background factored into obtaining success in your field of work?** I had fantastic professors at Purdue University who challenged my own perspectives and beliefs. They taught me to seek to understand and ask many questions. Growing into a continuous learner has contributed the most to my success, more than any field of study or what I chose as my major in college.

10. What was your greatest accomplishment as a professional? There are few experiences more powerful than making a wish come true. I've been able to contribute in my own small way to thousands of wishes in my career at Make-A-Wish, for which I am incredibly proud and grateful.

11. Why did you or do you work? I work because my skills and time can transform the life of a child with a critical illness. Knowing that is what makes me show up ready to do my best work every day.

12. What did you or do you value most about your occupation? Research shows that children who have wishes granted can build the physical and emotional strength they need to fight a critical illness. This may improve their quality of life and produce better health outcomes. Knowing that my daily work makes a tangible impact on a child is what I value most.

13. Please feel free to list any future projects you are working on you'd like to promote to list in this Plan B Book:

Make-A-Wish strives to someday grant the wish of every eligible child because wishes replace fear with confidence, anxiety with hope and sadness with joy. Although we grant more than 15,000 wishes a year, we estimate that close to twice that many kids annually are diagnosed with a qualifying condition. There is much more work to do if we want to bring the life-changing benefits of a wish-come-true to more kids with critical illnesses. Visit wish.org to learn how you can help make wishes come true.

SPORTS EQUIPMENT JOBS

50/50 Sales Representative ~ Account Executive ~ Account Manager ~ Account Marketing Manager ~ Accounts Payable Manager ~ Acquisition Creative Director ~ Ad Operations Coordinator ~ Adult Footwear Lead (Part-Time) ~ Agile Program Manager ~ America Brand Merchandise Manager ~ America Digital Business Development Manager ~ App Product Marketing Manager ~ App Senior Program Manager ~ Assistant Director of Marketing ~ Assistant General Manager ~ Assistant Manager Entertainment & Influencer Marketing ~ Assistant Sales Manager ~ Assistant Studio Manager ~ Assistant Volleyball Coach ~ Associate Director Marketing and Promotions ~ Associate IT Project Manager ~ Associate Product Manager ~ Athlete Concepts Director ~ Audio Account Executive ~ Basketball Director ~ Basketball Footwear Director ~ Brand Activation Manager ~ Brand Design Creative Producer ~ Brand Design Senior Designer ~ Brand Experience Specialist ~ Brand Manager ~ Brand Marketing Category Director ~ Brand Marketing Coordinator ~ Brand Marketing Operations Manager ~ Marketing Programs Specialist ~ Brand Member Service Manager ~ Brand Marketing Specialist ~ Budgeting Planning Coordinator ~ Business Analyst ~ Business Development Director ~ Business Director (Global Digital Commerce Operations & New Business) ~ Business Information Analyst ~ Business Planning Director ~ Category Marketing - Run Director ~ Clearance Store Product Lead ~ Club Operations Coordinator ~ College Sports Recruiting (Sales) ~ Communications Designer ~ Community Reporter/Sports Editor ~ Compliance Assistant Director ~ Consumer Sales Account Executive ~ Consumer Services Project Manager ~ Content and Copywriter ~ Content Licensing – Vice President ~ Content Marketing Coordinator ~ Copywriter ~ Copywriter – Digital Acquisition ~ Copywriter – Product Content ~ Corporate Sales Territory Manager ~ Creative Art Director ~ Creative Director ~ Creative Innovation Manager ~ Creative

Services Project Manager ~ Creative Studio Manager ~ Cross Category Digital Brand Manager ~ Custom Account Manager ~ Custom Product Associate ~ Cycling Program Manager ~ Data Analyst ~ Data Science Technical Lead ~ Demand Planner ~ Department Stores Account Manager ~ Design Assist ~ Design Director Environments ~ Design Lead (Premium) ~ Digital Account Manager ~ Digital & Innovation Policy Manager ~ Digital Analytics Senior Manager ~ Digital and Operations Sourcing Manager ~ Digital Commerce Design Manager ~ Digital Communications Manager ~ Digital Content Editor ~ Digital Content Producer ~ Digital Creative Director ~ Digital Designer ~ Digital Design Producer ~ Digital Footwear Engineer I ~ Digital Footwear Engineer I ~ Digital Marketing Associate Manager ~ Digital Marketing Director ~ Digital Marketing Innovation Manager ~ Digital Marketing Senior Manager ~ Digital Media Producer/Editor ~ Digital Product Analytics Manager ~ Digital Product Manager ~ Digital Production Manager ~ Digital Program Manager ~ Digital Project Manager ~ Digital Readiness Coordinator ~ Digital Senior Finance Analyst ~ Digital Video Content Producer ~ Director of Communications ~ Director of Creative Services ~ Director of Creative Video ~ Director of E Technical Delivery ~ Director of Golf ~ Director of Marketing ~ Director of Marketing & Strategy ~ Director of Premium Marketing ~ Director of Sales & Marketing ~ Director of Tickets and Marketing ~ Director Strategic Planning Global Brand ~ Director Strategy Activation ~ Director Technical Accounting & Policy ~ Direct Product Presentation Manager ~ District Vice-President ~ Ecommerce Content Specialist ~ Ecommerce Marketing Junior Manager ~ Email Marketing Manager ~ Email Marketing Senior Manager ~ Email Marketing Specialist ~ Engineering Program Director ~ Enterprise Architecture Program Manager ~ Enterprise Data Analyst ~ Entertainment Production Manager ~ Entry-Level Business Data Analyst ~ External Reporting Director ~ Events and Operations Manager ~ Events Coordinator ~ Event Services Assistant Manager ~ Events Vice-President ~ Fantasy Sports

Operations Manager ~ Fiber Transport Operations Manager ~ Finance Operations Manager ~ Fitness Sales Consultant ~ Fitness Service Manager ~ Football Director ~ Football Video Operations Manager ~ Footwear Color Designer I ~ Footwear Computational Designer I ~ Footwear Computational Designer II ~ Footwear Developer I ~ Footwear Lead ~ Footwear Product Manager ~ Footwear Purchasing Manager ~ Forecast Planning Manager ~ Frontline Service Delivery Manager ~ Full-Time Marketing Position ~ General Manager ~ General News/Sports Reporter ~ Global Account Executive ~ Global Benefits Business Analyst ~ Global Benefits Manager ~ Global Benefits Operations Analyst ~ Global Brand Communications Manager ~ Global Brand Design Senior Designer ~ Global Brand Merchandising Manager ~ Global Compensation Lead ~ Global Digital Marketing Manager ~ Global Digital Marketplace Development Manager ~ Global Direct Merchandise Sneakers Director ~ Global e-Commerce Operations Coordinator ~ Global Fan Insights Lead ~ Global L & D Instructional Designer ~ Global Marketing Manager ~ Global Media Distribution Director ~ Global Partnership Sales Director ~ Global Media Distribution Director ~ Global NBHD Senior Demand Planner ~ Global Product Manager (Road) ~ Global Product Vice President ~ Global Retail Design Manager ~ Global Software Asset Manager ~ Global Store Development Lead ~ Global Strategy Director ~ Global Strategy Vice-President ~ Global Trade & Logistics Specialist ~ Global Treasury Senior Manager ~ Global Visual Merchandising Producer ~ Golf Digital Merchandise Planner ~ Graphic Designer I ~ Group Events Account Executive ~ Group Sales Account Executive ~ Head of Global Marketing ~ Hockey Sticks Senior Manager ~ Human Resources Business Director ~ Human Resources Business Partner Senior Lead ~ Human Resources Operations Coordinator ~ Independent Sales Representative ~ Influencer Marketing Director ~ Initial Design Game Designer ~ Inside Sales Representative ~ Inside Sales Ticket Representative ~ Insights & Strategy Planner ~ Instrumentation Product Manager ~ Internal Communications Director ~ Internal

Communications Manager ~ Internal Communications Program Manager ~ Inventory Lead Product Manager ~ Investment Operations Coordinator ~ IT Business Analyst ~ Junior Copywriter ~ Junior Marketing Manager Opening ~ Lead Developer ~ Lead Instructor ~ Lead Report Developer ~ Lead Software Engineer ~ Learning Development Manager ~ Lead Personal Training Assistant Manager ~ Lifestyle Global Product Manager ~ Line Planning Product Director ~ Manager Campaign Operations (Responsible for Digital Content) ~ Manager Entertainment and Influencer Marketing ~ Manager of Communications ~ Manufacturing Planning Manager ~ Manufacturing Product Manager ~ Marketing and Sales Director ~ Marketing Analytics Manager ~ Marketing Coordinator ~ Marketing Data Analyst ~ Marketing Global Creative Director ~ Marketing Integration Specialist ~ Marketing Junior Manager ~ Marketing Lead ~ Marketing Manager ~ Marketing Programs Specialist ~ Marketing Specialist ~ Marketing Strategy Manager ~ Marketing Technical Manager ~ Master Data Analyst ~ Material Developer ~ Materials Developer I Footwear ~ Media Operations Manager ~ Media Sales Service Executive ~ Member Onboarding Manager ~ Member Services Account Manager ~ Membership Lead ~ Membership Sales Account Executive ~ Membership Sales Consultant ~ Membership Services Manager ~ Merchandise Manager ~ Mobile Marketing Senior Manager ~ Mountain Sports Product Manager ~ North America Strategy Director ~ Operations General Manager ~ Operations Manager ~ Outbound Logistics Supplier Relationship Manager ~ Outdoor Apparel Senior Design Lead ~ Outdoor Apparel Senior Design Manager ~ Outdoor Cycle Lead ~ Package Sales Account Executive ~ Part Time Distribution Specialist ~ Part-Time Research Analyst ~ Part-Time Sports Data Analyst ~ Partnership Marketing Coordinator ~ Performance Management Director ~ Premium Sales Account Executive ~ Process Manager/Product Owner ~ Producer (Creative Video)-Athletics ~ Product Advocate ~ Product Content Copywriter ~ Product Copywriter ~ Product Content Editor ~

Product Creation Delivery Manager ~ Product Design Engineer ~ Product Designer ~ Product Developer I ~ Product Developer II ~ Product Information Copywriter ~ Product Line Coordinator ~ Product Line Manager ~ Production Manager ~ Product Operations Manager ~ Product Operations Project Manager ~ Production Planner ~ Product Management Senior Manager ~ Product Marketing Coordinator ~ Production Operations Manager ~ Product Manager ~ Product Marketing Manager ~ Production Support Representative ~ Product Presentation Director ~ Product Systems Operations Lead ~ Production Planning Manager ~ Pro Football Assistant Equipment Manager ~ Pro Football Equipment Director ~ Pro Football Equipment/Field Assistant ~ Pro Football Equipment Manager ~ Pro Football Field Manager/Assistant Equipment Manager ~ Program Manager ~ Program Manager Digital Growth ~ Real Estate Development Director ~ Recruiting Coordinator ~ Retail Allocator ~ Retail Brand Manager ~ Retail Buyer ~ Retail Capabilities Program Manager ~ Retail Customer Service ~ Retail Divisional Vice-President ~ Retail Marketing Director ~ Retail Sales Associate ~ Retail Sales Manager ~ Retail Sales Spec Grove ~ Retail Sales Specialist ~ Retail Supervisor ~ Sales Associate ~ Sales Care Specialist ~ Sales Lead ~ Sales Manager ~ Sales/Marketing Associate ~ Sales Operations Coordinator ~ Sales Operations Manager ~ Sales Representative ~ Sales Specialist ~ Sales Support Representative ~ Sales Team Lead Hardlines ~ Sales Team Lead Softlines ~ Scheduling Operations Coordinator ~ Season Sales Account Executive ~ Seasonal Field Marketing Assistant ~ Seasonal Operations Coordinator ~ Senior Account Executive ~ Senior Brand Manager ~ Senior Business Analyst ~ Senior Business Data Analyst ~ Senior Client Operations Manager ~ Senior Copywriter ~ Senior Data Analyst ~ Senior Data Visualization Developer ~ Senior Designer Brand Design ~ Senior Digital Recruiter ~ Senior Director Sports Marketing ~ Senior Global Digital Analyst ~ Senior Graphics Designer – Team Sports Headquarters ~ Senior Information Security Specialist ~ Senior Marketing Activation Manager ~ Senior Marketing Manager ~ Senior

Material Developer ~ Senior Merchandiser ~ Senior Merchandiser (Softgoods) ~ Senior Post-Production Manager ~ Senior Producer/Editor ~ Senior Product Manager Retail Platform ~ Senior Product Marketing Manager ~ Senior Program Manager ~ Senior Regional Recruiter ~ Senior Retail Brand Experience Manager ~ Senior SAP Sales Business Analyst ~ Senior Software Digital Engineering ~ Senior Technical Developer ~ Senior Video Editor ~ Shift Production Manager ~ Site Coordinator ~ Ski Copywriter I ~ Social Marketing Associate Manager ~ Social Media Marketing Associate ~ Social Media Marketing Director ~ Social Media Senior Program Manager ~ Sponsorship Vice-President ~ Sports Account Executive ~ Sports Anchor/Multimedia Journalist ~ Sports Anchor/Reporter ~ Sports & Entertainment Talent Licensing Planner ~ Sports Broadcaster ~ Sport Content Video Editor ~ Sports Designer ~ Sports Editor ~ Sports Instructors ~ Sports Marketing Director ~ Sports Marketing Specialist ~ Sports Play by Play Board Operator ~ Sports Performance Specialist ~ Sports Scientist ~ Sports/Non-Sports Grader ~ Sports Site Manager ~ Sportswear Brand Manager ~ Sportswear Global Category Communications Director ~ Sportswear Strategic Planning Manager ~ Staffing Operations Manager ~ Stock Lead (Part-Time) ~ Store Inventory Control Team Lead ~ Store Logistics Manager ~ Store Sales Manager ~ Strategic Account Manager ~ Strategic Planning Manager ~ Studio Manager ~ Supervisor of Ecommerce Content ~ Supply Chain Analyst ~ Supply Chain Data Analyst ~ Talent Acquisition Vice-President ~ Team Account Executive ~ Team Account Manager ~ Team Sales Representative ~ Team Sports Footwear ~ Technical Developer I ~ Technical Developer II ~ Technical Lead ~ Technical Program Manager ~ Technical Specialist II ~ Temporary Digital Content Producer ~ Ticket Operations Coordinator ~ Ticket Sales Account Executive ~ Ticket Sales Representative ~ Track and Field Footwear Product Line Manager ~ Unified Sports Management ~ Vendor Management Manager ~ Venue Apps Product Manager ~ Video Cinematographer ~ Video Editor ~ Video Manager ~

Video Operations Manager ~ Video Producer ~ Video Product Manager ~ Video Producer & Editor ~ Visual Designer Digital Innovation ~ Volleyball Head Coach ~ Web Content Editor ~ Web Service Senior Product Manager ~ Website Marketing Specialist ~ Wholesale Marketing Coordinator.

STUDENT AND STUDENT-ATHLETE PLAN B BOOK
ALL STUDENTS, AND PARTICULARLY, STUDENT-ATHLETES, "DO YOU HAVE A PLAN B?"

Professional Occupation Profile for Student Academic & Career Developmental Exposure

PROFESSIONAL ATHLETE PROFILE – JOSH GIBSON

Josh Gibson is known by some baseball historians to be one of the greatest baseball players never to play in the major leagues. As a result of racial discrimination practices of that time period which were enforced against African Americans, Mr. Gibson excelled to become one of the greatest players to play in the professional Negro Baseball Leagues. He became known to many as the "Black Babe Ruth." Mr. Gibson was born and raised to the age of 13 in Buena Vista, Georgia. His family moved to Pittsburgh, PA in 1924 due to his father finding work in the steel mills. During his teenage years, he began vocational training to become an electrician. After working various jobs in that field, he began developing his athletic abilities while working, running track and playing baseball. He decided to focus on embarking on a semi-professional career in the sport of baseball. In 1927, that proved to be the year which catapulted him into the origin of his success as a rising star on the baseball diamond.

Mr. Gibson began his illustrious professional baseball career with the Homestead Grays of the Negro Baseball League in 1927. His successful introduction into the professional ranks proved to be a great decision to change his occupational direction to pursue his dream as a professional athlete. He batted .461 in his outstanding rookie season leading his team to the Eastern Divisional Championship. After spending four seasons with the Homestead Grays, in which, he lead his team with 75 home runs, Mr. Gibson left the team to join the Pittsburgh Crawfords.

As a member of the Pittsburgh Crawfords, Mr. Gibson experienced some of his greatest accomplishments in baseball with this team. He batted one season with an average of .467, another season he hit 84 home runs, and he piled up numerous all-star selections as a standout catcher and power hitter. Mr. Gibson and fellow all-star pitcher, Satchel Page, who would later go on to play in professional baseball's Major Leagues, both played for the Pittsburgh Crawfords which was known to be one of the best teams of all-time. Josh Gibson's talents were, also, respected worldwide which led him to play in Cuba and Mexico, as well as other countries. Furthermore, Gibson left to play baseball for two years in the Dominican Republic and Puerto Rico before returning to play with the Homestead Grays for the next nine seasons. The next nine seasons produced total dominance by his team as they won nine straight Negro League Championships.

Mr. Gibson's baseball career spanned over a 17 year period. He was believed to have amassed nearly 800 home runs, a career batting average of over .350, and he was a nine-time all-star (while batting .483 in all-star games). He was viewed by many Major League players, such as, Walter Johnson who played against him during exhibition games with the Negro League teams, as one of the best baseball players of all-time whether a black or white player. It is believed that Josh Gibson had a batting average of .426 against Major League pitchers. Due to Josh Gibson's exemplary accomplishments in the ballparks across baseball diamonds throughout the world, he was elected into the National Baseball Hall of Fame in 1972.

He was a man and athlete before his time which provided a foundation for African-American baseball players. His life was to be taken seriously as physically, athletically, mentally and proficient enough of a talent to be accepted into the Major Leagues as a qualified participant within their association as a "human being." Even though Josh Gibson did not play in the Major Leagues due to racial segregation in professional baseball at the time, his contributions to baseball became the foundation and impetus to aspiring African-American student-athletes. This allowed them the opportunity of obtaining the "field of dreams" they can now pursue, as a result of his athletic exploits. Josh Gibson's successes in professional baseball during his playing days in the Negro Leagues and leagues throughout the world was evident to the Major Leagues that African-Americans were able and ready to enter their game. As a result, Mr. Gibson helped to open doors of opportunities for other African-American baseball players to play in the Major Leagues such as the first African-American baseball player allowed to play in the Major Leagues which was Jackie Robinson.

Josh Gibson tragically lost his wife while she was in childbirth early on in his baseball career. The birth produced twin children who both survived. Mr. Gibson was able to continue his baseball career as he provided for his family. However, he began to experience some health hardships as he progressed in the later days of his baseball career. He was diagnosed with a brain tumor, but that didn't stop him from continuing to excel on the baseball field. He earned two more batting titles and three more home run titles despite having numerous headaches and dizziness spells as he played. After his death in 1947 at the age of 35, he still received recognition and honor for the outstanding feats he accomplished as an athlete. In addition to being named to the National Baseball Hall of Fame in Cooperstown, New York, he has been celebrated through the following: statues to his honor, his childhood baseball field was named after him, a Pittsburgh opera was created called *The Summer King* about his life to highlight his significance, a scholastic and athletic foundation was created in his memory called The Josh Gibson Foundation, and the Nike Sporting Goods Company recognized him by developing the first signature shoe for a Negro League player. African-Americans, as well as, all Americans can be proud of the sacrifices and accomplishments that propelled Josh Gibson to such lofty heights which, in turn, elevated our entire society to that same spectacular level of equality for all.

STUDENT AND STUDENT-ATHLETE PLAN B BOOK
ALL STUDENTS, AND PARTICULARLY, STUDENT-ATHLETES, "DO YOU HAVE A PLAN B?

Professional Occupation Questionnaire for Student Academic & Career Developmental Exposure

Name: Sean L. Gibson

Your Current Job Title and/or the Job You're Most Known for Participating: Executive director of Josh Gibson Foundation

Number of Years in Current Position or Number of Years in the Position You're Most Known for Participating: 17 years

List the Previous Job Titles You've Had: Residence counselor at The Academy

List College Major(s), Master Degree(s), Doctoral Degree(s): Edinboro University degree in Criminal Justice

1. **Who inspired you the most?** My Grandfather, Josh Gibson, Jr inspired me the most. He was a father figure to me who taught me right from wrong, the "dos" and the "don'ts" which was instrumental in my upbringing.

2. **What motivated you during the pursuit of your career?** Coming from public housing and a single parent home were the motivating factors for giving me the drive I needed to seek after a career for myself. I wanted to get out of the "hood." Not to say that the "hood" was a bad place, but I wanted something

different for my kids. I focused on obtaining a college degree through playing basketball, in which, I was successfully able to accomplish this goal.

3. **Who or what influenced you to achieve your goal(s) as a professional?** Several people were influential during my developmental process of becoming a professional. The following people influenced me most: George Miles – head of the WQED television station was a mentor to me, my college friends provided beneficial guidance as I was getting closer to graduation, Clarence Curry –a professor at California University of Pennsylvania gave me great advice for participating in non-profit work, my cousin Ron Carter attended VMI University and played basketball for the L.A. Lakers, and he was of great help in contributing to my overall development as a person, and my cousin Petty Gibson played basketball at New Mexico State University, and he was a really good person to look up to as role model. These people were all essential in my life because they were people who you could have a conversation with to open up your mind to different perspectives and opportunities which enabled me to grow as a person in all areas of life.

4. **What goal(s) did you set for yourself in attempting to reach your career aspiration(s)?** My first goal was aimed at getting the foundation started in the non-profit organization spectrum of business. Our foundation had to devise a plan the following: to get funding, develop an educational program, create a baseball & sports curriculum program, generate fundraisers, implement an advertising campaign to

familiarize our foundation's name more in the public, focus on managing well the good programs and products the organization originated, concentrate on fostering positive business relationships while keeping them in good standing for possible future engagements, cultivate partnerships with other organizations, and I endeavored to create programs for kids who are in need. Some of the foundation's primary goals are designed to get kids off the street, and into programs that can help to build them up on the inside to utilize their talents and abilities to make them more prepared for the future.

5. **What were your greatest strengths that you executed as a professional within your career?**
As a professional, my greatest strength is the connection that I develop with people. It's not what you know, but it is who you know. The conversation that we have with people is vital to establishing relationships that can benefit each person. Through connecting in conversations with people, it afforded me the opportunity to help others achieve their goals. Always give back with whatever you can, such as: giving people your time, your advice and your money to help other people reach their greatest potential. Remember, in life, you'll never get ahead unless you give back to help someone else. It's vital to be a people person. I believe another important strength that I possess is the ability to speak in a professional manner. Therefore, it is very important to learn in English class how to speak grammatically correct.

6. **What most challenged you during your journey to becoming the professional in your occupation?** Getting started in the non-profit field was a challenge, especially, because I studied criminal justice in college. So, transitioning into a new business environment took extensive research and time to learn a new industry. When my grandfather asked me to run our family's foundation, I wanted to represent our family the best way I could by helping to leave a legacy. Our legacy had to emphasize the core values of our beliefs while enriching the lives of the youth from our community. As a result of taking on this challenge, I received a valuable lesson only begotten from taking on this new responsibility. My experience with my family's foundation has shown me that, in life, sometimes you have to step out and take a risk, especially, when you are starting something new.

7. **How did you manage your weaknesses within your occupation?** I managed my weaknesses by looking to others to pull me up when I was in need of help. I sought after the help of mentors and peers of mine to receive of the strengths that they possessed to assist me in overcoming my weakness. This process led me to succeed and overcome in the areas where I was weak by turning my weaknesses into strengths.

8. **How important was time management in performing well on your job?** Time management is very important, and it is key to performing well in life. It's especially important when you're in school because you have to come up with a schedule for yourself that prioritizes your homework, study time,

social life and activities to allow for you to be as successful as possible. When you're working, and you have a meeting, then you have to plan for the following: how long it takes you to get to your meeting, how much work you need to finish before the meeting, you have to know what you are to do in the meeting and what is needed for you to bring to the meeting. So, there is a lot of planning and scheduling that needs to be done, in order, to function optimally with your time. Developing a routine when you're in school or working on a daily basis will help a lot with time management while you're learning. At the same time, you need to be able to amend and/or change your schedule when it is necessary.

9. **How much of your educational background factored into obtaining success in your field of work?** My educational background in criminal justice helped later on in my career. I was able to help kids by informing them of the keys to living a law-abiding type of life. This was as an integral component to staying focused as these kids journeyed toward achieving their goals.

10. **What was your greatest accomplishment as a professional?** The greatest accomplishments within our foundation to date are as follows: in 2008, $500,000 was used to renovate a Pittsburgh baseball field where Josh Gibson played as a boy to be renamed in his honor the Josh Gibson Field, the Pittsburgh Opera created a production called *The Summer King* which is based on the life and accomplishments of Josh Gibson, the Nike sporting goods company came

out with the Josh Gibson signature shoe in 2009, and a statue of Josh Gibson was erected in Washington DC to honor him and other great Negro League baseball players.

11. **Why did you or do you work?** I work for the following reasons: to continue the legacy of my family, the accomplishments of my great grandfather Josh Gibson, Sr., provide an educational background of the significance of the African American Negro Baseball League and its impact on the American Sports culture, and also, teaching the history of African American Black History 365 days a year. Additionally, I work to provide a living for my family financially. I, also, view work as a gift, because I get to share a rich history that is so important to the fabric of the origin of this country's national past-time.

12. **What did you or do you value most about your occupation?** Legacy is number one and of the utmost importance to me. Our family name is so important that I teach my kids that it is to be respected and reflected upon how you are to live your life and represent your family. We must always be mindful of how our actions speak to the lives we project in society. My grandfather, Josh Gibson, Jr., picked me to run the foundation, and I respect and honor his choice to choose me. So, I am extremely grateful and honored to lead the family foundation, and I will endeavor to make my family proud.

13. **Future Projects:** In the year of 2020 in downtown Pittsburgh, statues of Negro players (which include Josh Gibson Sr.) will be erected as a memorial park to honor their groundbreaking accomplishments with a $1.2 million project. It is currently under construction to celebrate the 100 year anniversary of the origin of the Negro Baseball League. The Josh Gibson Foundation features the BOSA curriculum which is a sports and education program. It involves high school students from 10th to 12th grades who participate in high school level courses geared towards careers which count toward college credits. Additionally, one of the future goals of the Josh Gibson Foundation is to own its own facility.

14. **Last Word of Encouragement to the youth:**
Students, it is vital that you stay positive, and you need to be physically active by getting daily exercise. Spend more time focused on moving and less time focused on using social media.

STUDENT AND STUDENT-ATHLETE PLAN B BOOK
ALL STUDENTS, AND PARTICULARLY, STUDENT-ATHLETES, "DO YOU HAVE A PLAN B?

Professional Occupation Questionnaire for Student Academic & Career Developmental Exposure

Name: Ervin Rogers, Jr.

Your Current Job Title and/or the Job You're Most Known for Participating: Associate (Structural Engineer)
Number of Years in Current Position or Number of Years in the Position You're Most Known for Participating: 2 yrs (17 years)

List the Previous Job Titles You've Had: Project Manager; Structural engineer; Project engineer

List College Major(s), Master Degree(s), Doctoral Degree(s): Bachelor in Science (B.S.) in Civil Engineering, Professional Masters in Engineering

1. **Who inspired you the most?** My inspiration can be credited to my father.

2. **What motivated you during the pursuit of your career?** I took a class in middle school that exposed me to the engineering field. During high school, I decided to go in the direction of civil engineering.

3. **Who or what influenced you to achieve your goal(s) as a professional?** My dad motivated me to get my master's degree because he had one and his work ethic was also influential. Furthermore, I was motivated to be successful in anything I did.

4. **What goal(s) did you set for yourself in attempting to reach your career aspiration(s)?** My first goal was to get my master's degree after finishing the undergraduate program. Passing the exam to receive a professional engineering license was my next goal. After receiving my professional engineering license, I planned to become an associate with a firm. My final goal is to become a partner at a firm.

5. **What were your greatest strengths that you executed as a professional within your career?** Two of my greatest strengths are my willingness to learn something new for my career and to learn from others. I am, also, skilled with the ability to problem solve. Lastly, I'm able to visualize things in 3D.

6. **What most challenged you during your journey to becoming the professional in your occupation?** Understanding the politics that are involved in the work I do, is what challenged me most. You need to be very careful and calculated in terms of how you handle situations or you may cost yourself future work or projects.

7. **How did you manage your weaknesses within your occupation?** First, you need to be honest with yourself and identify your weaknesses. After that, I worked hard to do better in those areas. I usually take my time and take a step back when situations arise that I am weak in those capacities. I have also learned to defer situations to others that are stronger than me and learn from how they handle things.

8. **How important was time management in performing well on your job?** It helps a lot since I handle multiple projects. The only issue with time management is that you can only be as good with it as those above you.

9. **How much of your educational background factored into obtaining success in your field of work?** Education in the field of engineering provides you with the understanding, concepts, and theories about what you do on the job. As a result, it shows if you have the aptitude and way of thinking required to be competent in this line of work.

10. **What was your greatest accomplishment as a professional?** Passing the professional engineering exam to get my license and becoming an associate at my firm was my greatest accomplishment.

11. **Why did you or do you work?** I like the challenges that my job presents to me. I enjoy mentoring the younger engineers the way I was mentored by my mentor.

12. **What did you or do you value most about your occupation?** I value the challenges and seeing a project completed. I always get enjoyment when a project I designed and managed is completed.

SPORTS MANAGEMENT JOBS

50/50 Sales Representative ~ Accounting Assistant ~ Account Marketing Manager ~ Administration Assistant ~ Administration Assistant (Seasonal) ~ Affiliate Marketing Coordinator ~ App Product Marketing Manager ~ Assistant Business Manager ~ Assistant Clubhouse Manager ~ Assistant General Manager ~ Assistant Groundskeeper ~ Assistant Manager ~ Assistant Marketing Coordinator ~ Assistant Sales Director ~ Assistant Sales Manager ~ Associate Product Manager ~ Brand Marketing Manager ~ Business Office – Assistant Director ~ Buyer ~ Client Partner Vice President ~ Content Marketing Specialist ~ Content Strategy Vice President ~ Digital Marketing Manager ~ Ecommerce Junior Marketing Manager ~ Elite Athlete Services Coordinator ~ Email Marketing Specialist ~ Event Coordinator ~ Events Operations Associate ~ Event Sales Director ~ Events Sales Manager ~ Event Time Ticket Sales Staff ~ Food and Nutrition Editor ~ General Manager ~ Global Digital Marketing Manager ~ Graphics Production Assistant ~ Group Sales Account Executive ~ Group Sales Specialist ~ Human Resources Business Partner Senior Manager ~ Human Resources Vice President ~ Independent Sales Representative ~ Influencer Marketing Director ~ Inside Sales Representative ~ Inside Sales Ticket Representative ~ Junior Marketing Manager ~ League Coordinator ~ Marketing Programs Specialist ~ Marketing Specialist ~ Marketing Vice President ~ Materials Coordinator ~ Merchandising – Assistant Manager ~ National Sales Manager ~ New Product Development Associate ~ Product Marketing Manager ~ Product Operations Associate ~ Operations Associate ~ Operations Coordinator ~ Operations Leader ~ Operations Manager ~ Operations Vice President ~ Partnership Strategy Coordinator ~ Premium Sales Representative ~ Product Systems Operations Lead ~ Production Coordinator ~ Program Manager ~ Regional Sales Manager ~ Retail Buyer ~

Retail Sales Manager ~ Retail Sales Specialist ~ Sales/Account Manager ~ Sales Associate ~ Sales Manager ~ Sales Operations Associate ~ Sales Operations Manager ~ Sales Representative ~ Sales Specialist ~ Sales Support Representative ~ Seasonal Video Assistant ~ Security Vice President ~ Senior Indirect Buyer ~ Senior Manager Brand Marketing ~ Senior Marketing Manager ~ Senior Retail Brand Experience Manager ~ Senior Security Specialist ~ Senior Specialist Retail Marketing ~ Senior Video Editor ~ Show Car Coordinator ~ Site Production Coordinator ~ Social Video Producer/Editor ~ Sports Editor ~ Sports Marketing Assistant Manager ~ Sports Senior Editor ~ Social Coordinator ~ Store Sales Manager ~ Talent Buyer Vice President ~ Team Sales Representative ~ Team Vice President of Marketing ~ Territory Sales Manager ~ Territory Sales Representative ~ Ticket Sales General Manager ~ Ticket Sales Manager ~ Ticket Sales Representative ~ Trade Marketing Specialist ~ Vice President of Operations ~ Video Coordinator ~ Video Editor ~ Video Operations Manager ~ Web-based Editor ~ Website Marketing Manager ~ Website Marketing Specialist.

STUDENT AND STUDENT-ATHLETE PLAN B BOOK
ALL STUDENTS, AND PARTICULARLY, STUDENT-ATHLETES, "DO YOU HAVE A PLAN B?

Professional Occupation Questionnaire for Student Academic & Career Developmental Exposure

Name: Robert Jackson

Your Current Job Title and/or the Job You're Most Known for Participating: Northeast Regional Talent Scout for San Antonio Spurs of the National Basketball Association (NBA)

Number of Years in Current Position or Number of Years in the Position You're Most Known for Participating: 14 years

List the Previous Job Titles You've Had: Basketball: High School Coach, College Head Coach, and College Assistant Coach

List College Major(s), Master Degree(s), Doctoral Degree(s): Bachelor Degree in Physical Education, Associate Degree in Health, Physical Education and Recreation from Northeastern University.

1. **Who inspired you the most?** Both of my parents were most inspirational to me, especially my mother.

2. **What motivated you during the pursuit of your career?** First and foremost, getting a college education motivated me most, as well as, being able to obtain a satisfying career.

3. **Who or what influenced you to achieve your goal(s) as a professional?** As I watched my parents work extremely hard, and never making any excuses, is what influenced my desires to achieve my goals.

4. **What goal(s) did you set for yourself in attempting to reach your career aspiration(s)?** Being the very best person I could be, respecting everyone and obtaining a college degree, which was absolutely imperative, were the goals I set for myself.

5. **What were your greatest strengths that you executed as a professional within your career?** The greatest strengths that I performed as a professional were being a hard-working employee that executed my position within the workplace at a high level of professionalism.

6. **What most challenged you during your journey to becoming the professional in your occupation?** Beating the odds by having to constantly prove myself was my biggest challenge.

7. **How did you manage your weaknesses within your occupation?** I eventually made my weaknesses my strengths.

8. **How important was time management in performing well on your job?** I had a rule my whole life to arrive 30 minutes early for work, as well as staying late. I believed this produced quality over quantity in regards to my work performance.

9. **How much of your educational background factored into obtaining success in your field of work?** Education certainly helped, but networking was certainly a key component too.

10. What was your greatest accomplishment as a professional? Receiving a scouting position with the San Antonio Spurs in the NBA was my greatest accomplishment as a professional.

11. Why did you or do you work? I work to survive and to have ownership of what I need in life.

12. What did you or do you value most about your occupation? Valuing the fact that I have an opinion, and not being afraid to be wrong is what's most significant about my occupation.

13. Additional comments to encourage the youth: The one defining moment along my professional journey occurred when I was told that it would be virtually impossible for me to land an NBA job. Instead of believing it, and giving up, those remarks made me more determined and driven. It's never easy to accomplish your goals, so being a very hard worker will always pay off. Always remember to be prepared, because it is good to have the mindset that you never know who is watching you.

SPORTS PROFESSIONAL PROFILE
ALL STUDENTS, AND PARTICULARLY, STUDENT-ATHLETES, "DO YOU HAVE A PLAN B?

Professional Occupation Questionnaire for Student Academic & Career Developmental Exposure

Name: Dr. Keith Henschen

Your Current Job Title and/or the Job You're Most Known for Participating: Emeritus Professor of the Department of Exercise and Sports Sciences at the University of Utah

Number of Years in Current Position or Number of Years in the Position You're Most Known for Participating: over 38 years

List the Previous Job Titles You've Had: Applied Sport Psychology practitioner with the Utah Jazz of the NBA for over 30 years, USA Track & Field, USA Gymnastics, U.S. Aerials Alpine Ski Team, U.S. Speed Skating Teams, U.S. Men's Alpine Ski Team, The University of Utah Athletic Department, BYU Athletic Department, Consultant for a number of U.S. Olympic Teams and athletes

List College Major(s), Master Degree(s), Doctoral Degree(s): Bachelor Degree in Sports Psychology from Ball State University, Master's Degree in Sports Psychology from Saint Francis College, Doctoral Degree in Sports Psychology from Indiana University

1. **Who inspired and influenced you to achieve your goal(s) as a professional the most?** I have been inspired most by my high school coach, Mr. Byard Hey.

2. What motivated you during the pursuit of your career?
Julie D. Henschen (wife) has been my constant companion for 49+ years and has provided inspiration for whatever I have accomplished in the era of performance psychology. Also, my graduate students have been my inspiration who have taught me more than I have taught them.

3. What goal(s) did you set for yourself in attempting to reach your career aspiration(s)? My goal was to become a college professor in the field of sports psychology.

4. What were your greatest strengths that you executed as a professional within your career? My greatest strength was being a challenging teacher.

5. What most challenged you during your journey to becoming the professional in your occupation? In 1971, I received my doctorate from Indiana University and accepted a position at the University of Utah with the challenge to develop a graduate program in the psychological aspects of sports. The field (sports psychology) was relatively new and just emerging in higher education. I realized that I had a lot to learn, and I was excited about the challenge. I believe my competitiveness learned in sports from an early age, readily transferred to academics was the motivation I needed to excel. My sports background has allowed me insight into the nuances of the mental aspects of performance as well as to "talk the language" of performers. My training in psychology and counseling has taught me to listen adroitly and thus identify the real issues that frequently confront the struggling performer. In my case, the following old adage is very appropriate: "We are when we are old what we learn when we are young!"

6. How much of your educational background factored into obtaining success in your field of work?
All of my educational training has factored into obtaining success in my field of work.

7. What was your greatest accomplishment as a professional?

My greatest accomplishments as a professional were being voted to be the President of the American Alliance for Health, Physical Education, Recreation and Dance (AAHPERD) for two years, and I was, also, voted to be the President of the International Society of Sports Psychology for six years.

8. What did you value most about your occupation and did you work?
What I value most about my occupation is my ability to teach, working with professional athletes, and being on the staff of 10 Olympic teams is what makes working so worthwhile.

9. Please feel free to read the excellent book entitled: *Don't Leave Your Mind Behind (The Mental Side of Performance)* authored by Dr. Keith Henshcen with Dr. Nicole Detling

SPORTS MEDIA JOBS

3D Animator ~ Account Executive (Inside Sales) ~ Account Manager ~ Acquisition Marketing Manager ~ Ad Operations Manager ~ Ad Solutions Coordinator ~ Advanced Marketing Product Manager ~ Advanced Media Manager ~ Advertising & Program Coordinator West Coast ~ Adobe Premiere Junior Editor/Preditor ~ Affiliate Relations Manager ~ Animator ~ Apparel Digital Product Director ~ Apparel Production Analyst ~ Apparel Production Assistant ~ Application and Help Desk Support ~ Assistant Director Marketing and Promotions ~ Assistant Director of Sales ~ Assistant Manager ~ Assistant Sales Director ~ Assistant Superintendent ~ Assisting Managing Editor ~ Associate Creative Designer ~ Associate Designer Motion Graphics ~ Associate Digital Producer ~ Associate Editor (NFL) ~ Associate Graphic Designer ~ Associate IT Project Manager ~ Associate Producer ~ Associate Producer II ~ Associate Producer I (Part-Time) ~ Associate Producer II (Part-Time) ~Associate Producer (Sports) ~ Associate Project Manager ~ Associate Technical Producer ~ Associate Video Producer ~ Audience Development Manager ~ Audio Operator ~ Avid Editor ~ AV Support Specialist ~ Bilingual Sports Content Researcher ~ Board Operator On-Call ~ Board Operator/Tape Operator ~ Branded Content Associate Producer ~ Branded Content Senior Producer ~ Brand Marketing Director ~ Brand Marketing Manager ~ Broadcast Operations Manager (BOC) ~ Broadcast Operations Senior Manager ~ Budgeting Planning Coordinator ~ Business Analyst ~ Business Development Sports Manager ~ Business Operations Assistant AD ~ Business Operations Analyst ~ Business Operations Manager ~ Business Performance Analyst ~ Camera Operator Studio Technician ~ Category Sales Director ~ Client Service Coordinator ~ Client Services Director ~ Client Services Representative ~ Club Development Program Coach ~ Club Digital Strategy

Coordinator ~ Club Operations Coordinator ~ College Sports Video Editor ~ Communications Coordinator ~ Community Affairs Trainee ~ Community Impact Senior Manager ~ Community Moderator ~ Community Partnerships Manager ~ Community Reporter/Sports Editor ~ Computer Graphics Operator ~ Content Analytics Senior Manager ~ Content Associate ~ Content Business Operations Director ~ Content Coordinator ~ Content Marketing Vice President ~ Content Miner (Reports to the Senior Editor helping to find publishing and promoting content) ~ Content Producer ~ Content Producer/Editor Films ~ Content/Social Media Manager ~ Content Strategy Vice-President ~ Continuity Manager ~ Coordinator of Marketing ~ Coordinating Marketing Editor ~ Coordinator of Athletic Multimedia ~ Coordinator of Video Services ~ Corp Development Financial Analyst ~ Corporate Account Manager ~ Creative Art Director ~ Cross Cultural Marketing Manager ~ Cross Platform Sales Director ~ CRM Marketing Analyst ~ Cycle Club Coordinator ~ Data Engineer ~ Data Ingestion Product Manager ~ Data Platform Product Manager (Advanced TV) ~ Data Product Manager ~ Data Science Manager ~ Data Science Technical Lead ~ Data Senior Product Manager ~ Data Visualization Engineer ~ Demand Generation Vice President ~ Deportes Marketing Coordinator (US Hispanic) ~ Design Director ~ Digital Account Manager ~ Digital Acquisition Copywriter ~ Digital Acquisition Senior Director ~ Digital Affiliate & Distribution Manager ~ Digital & Social Analysis Manager ~ Digital Associate Producer I ~ Digital Business Analyst ~ Digital Business Planning Director ~ Digital Campaign Manager ~ Digital Catalog Coordinator ~ Digital Communications Manager ~ Digital Content Coordinator ~ Digital Content Manager ~ Digital Content Producer ~ Digital Creative Director ~ Digital Creative Project Manager ~ Digital Desk Manager ~ Digital Distribution & Growth Senior Manager ~ Digital Editor in Chief ~ Digital Graphic Designer ~ Digital Human Resources Director ~ Digital Marketing Associate ~ Digital Marketing Coordinator ~ Digital Marketing Associate Manager ~ Digital Marketing Manager ~ Digital Marketing

Senior Manager ~ Digital Marketplace Director ~ Digital Media and Art Producer ~ Digital Media Coordinator ~ Digital Media Manager ~ Digital Media Producer/Editor ~ Digital Merchandising Ecommerce Manager ~ Digital Planning Director ~ Digital Product Analytics Manager ~ Digital Product Manager ~ Digital Production Analytics Manager ~ Digital Production Manager ~ Digital Research Analyst ~ Digital Retail Planning Director ~ Digital Signage Technician ~ Digital Sports Director ~ Digital Video Content Producer ~ Digital Video Producer ~ Digital Video Seasonal Assistant ~ Digital Video Specialist ~ Digital/Web Project Manager ~ Director I ~ Director of Athletic Event Management ~ Director of Athletics ~ Director of Communications ~ Director of Community Programs ~ Director of Data Visualization ~ Director of Delivery & Support ~ Director of Digital Innovation ~ Director of Golf Operations ~ Director of People & Culture ~ Director of Programming ~ Director of Sales ~ Director of Ticket Sales ~ Director of Marketing ~ Director Online Media ~ Distinctive Events Coordinator ~ Distribution House Purchasing Coordinator ~ Division Manager ~ E-Commerce Category Manager ~ E-commerce Graphic Designer II ~ E-commerce Web and Digital Analyst ~ Editor ~ Editorial Producer ~ Email Marketing Analyst ~ Email Marketing Coordinator ~ Email Marketing Manager ~ Email Marketing Professional ~ Email Marketing Senior Manager ~ Embroidery Operator ~ Engineering Project Coordinator ~ Equipment Design Director ~ Executive Producer/Original Content ~ Event & Marketing Manager (Culture) ~ Event Coordinator Athlete Liaison ~ Event Production Director ~ Event Sales Administrator ~ Event Sales Director ~ Event Sales Manager ~ Events Coordinator ~ Event Security Manager ~ EVS Operator ~ Facilities Coordinator ~ Fan Relations Ticket Agent ~ Fantasy Baseball Sabermetric Analyst ~ Fantasy Sports Product Manager ~ Female Hockey Coordinator ~ FIFA Assistant Content Producer ~ Finance Analyst ~ Finance Operations Analyst ~ Financial Analyst ~ Financial Analyst II ~ Financial Analyst III ~ Financial Reporting

Product Owner ~ Financial Wholesale Senior Analyst ~ Fitness Manager ~ Fitness Specialist ~ Food and Nutrition Editor ~ Freelance Digital Producer/Editor ~ Freelance Director ~ Freelance Network Operator ~ Freelance/Part-Time Ticker Copy Editor ~ Freelance Production Assistant ~ Frontline Service Delivery Manager ~ Fundraising Coordinator ~ Game Operations Associate ~ Games Event and IP Management Manager ~ Games Event Management Manager ~ General Ledger Accountant ~ General News/Sports Reporter ~ Global Benefits Manager ~ Global Benefits Operations Analyst ~ Global Brand Merchandising Manager ~ Global Digital Marketing Manager ~ Marketing Strategy Coordinator ~ Global Media Distribution Associate ~ Global Media Operations Associate ~ Global Partnership Sales Manager ~ Global Partnerships Manager ~ Global Product Manager – Road ~ Global Retail Design Manager ~ Global Treasury Senior Manager ~ Golfer Care Specialist ~ Golfer Support Agent ~ Golf Sales Associate ~ Graphic Designer ~ Graphics Production Assistant ~ Group Sales Specialist ~ Group Service Coordinator ~ Head of Global Marketing ~ Head of Marketing ~ Health Fitness Program Manager ~ Highlight Producer ~ Human Resources Associate ~ Human Resources Coordinator ~ Human Resources Director ~ Human Resources Generalist ~ Human Resources Manager ~ Human Resources Manager Agile Resource ~ Human Resources Operations Coordinator ~ Human Resources Senior Administrator Assistant ~ Human Resources Specialist – Part Time ~ Human Resources Strategic Partner ~ Human Resources Technology Manager ~ Human Resources Vice President ~ Image Editor ~ In-Game Social Media Coordinator ~ Injest Operator I ~ In-Store Marketing Manager ~ Inventory Lead Product Manager ~ IT Business Analyst ~ IT Retail Support Analyst ~ IT Support Specialist ~ Junior Graphic Designer ~ Junior Marketing Manager Opening ~ Junior Project Manager ~ Launch Support Analyst ~ Lead Content Strategist ~ Lead Image Editor ~ Lead Media Operator (Part-Time) ~ Lead Mobile Engineer ~ Lead Product Analyst ~ Lead Studio/Camera

Operator ~ Lead Technical Director ~ Lead Technical Recovery Analyst ~ League Coordinator ~ Learning & Development Specialist I ~ Live Content Producer ~ Live Event Sports Producer ~ Local Sports Coach ~ Loyalty Business Analyst ~ Manager Data Platform Product (Advanced TV) ~ Manager of Athletic Media Relations ~ Manager of Event Sales ~ Manager of Sports Officials ~ Managing Producer ~ Manufacturing Planning Manager ~ Manufacturing Product Manager ~ Marketing Analytics Manager ~ Marketing Coordinator ~ Marketing Director or Coordinator ~ Marketing - Ecomm Junior Manager ~ Marketing Manager ~ Marketing Planner ~ Marketing Program Coordinator ~ Marketing Senior Director ~ Marketing Strategy Coordinator ~ Marketing Technical Manager ~ Market Research Analyst ~ Market Sales Manager ~ Media Board Operator ~ Media Coordinator ~ Media Operations Workflow Associate ~ Media Product Marketing Analyst ~ Media Video Producer ~ Member Onboarding Manager ~ Member Services Associate ~ Membership Product Manager ~ Membership Sales Advisor ~ Membership Sales Consultant ~ Merchandise Account Manager ~ Metabolic Specialist ~ MLB Video Editor ~ Motions Graphic Designer ~ Mountain Sports Product Manager ~ Multimedia Journalist Sports ~ Multimedia Sports Reporter ~ Multi-Platform Coordinator ~ Multi-Platform Editor ~ Multi-Platform Producer ~ National Sales - Sports & Olympics Director ~ NCAA Account Manager ~ News and Sports On Call Producer ~ News Assistant ~ Night Homepage Editor ~ Night Side Graphics Designer ~ Nutrition Program Coordinator ~ Nutrition Program Lead ~ Omnichannel Drop Ship Analyst ~ On-Air Board Operator ~ On-Air Graphics Operator ~ On Air Promos- Writer/Editor/Producer ~ On Call Board Operator ~ Operations Associate ~ Operations Financial Analyst ~ Operations Manager ~ Operations Research Manager ~ Operations Training Manager ~ Oracle Business Analyst ~ Paid Media Strategy Manager ~ Paint Booth Operator ~ Partnerships Account Manager ~ Partnership Solutions Specialist ~ Partnership Strategy

Coordinator ~ Part-Time Bilingual Editor ~ Part-Time Camera Operator ~ Part-Time CG Operator ~ Part-Time Circulation Coordinator ~ Part-Time Photo Coordinator ~ Part-Time Research Analyst ~ Part-Time Resource Coordinator (Studio Directing) ~ Part-Time Sales Leader ~ Part-Time Sports Content Researcher ~ Part-Time Web Content Editor ~ People Team Director (Human Resources) ~ PEP Associate Producer (Produces Highlights & Features) ~ PEP Production Assistant (Produces Highlights & Features) ~ Photo Digital Editor ~ Pilates Coordinator ~ Planning Analyst ~ Platform Preditor ~ Playout Operator ~ Posting & Toasting Contributor ~ Premium Service Coordinator ~ Principal Engineer ~ Product Alignment Manager ~ Product Analyst ~ Producer/Editor ~ Product Architect ~ Product Content Editor ~ Product Creation Delivery Manager ~ Product Data Product Director ~ Product Design Director ~ Product Development & Production Assistant Manager ~ Product Information Editor ~ Product Line Coordinator ~ Product Management Manager ~ Product Management Senior Manager ~ Product Manager ~ Product Marketing Analyst ~ Product Merchant Manager ~ Product Merchant Manager II ~ Product Merchant Manager III ~ Product Safety Analyst ~ Product Support ~ Production Assistant ~ Production Assistant (Bilingual) ~ Production Coordinator I ~ Production Operations Manager ~ Production Planner ~ Production Scheduling Coordinator ~ Production Supervisor ~ Production Support Representative ~ Pro Baseball Apparel Digital Product Director ~ Pro Baseball Content Marketing Specialist ~ Pro Baseball Digital Content Associate ~ Pro Baseball Digital Content Coordinator ~ Pro Baseball Digital Content Producer ~ Pro Baseball Digital Content Specialist ~ Pro Baseball Digital Signage Technician ~ Pro Baseball DTC Capabilities Director ~ Pro Baseball Ecommerce Content Specialist ~ Pro Baseball Digital Marketplace Director ~ Pro Baseball Temporary Digital Content Producer ~ Pro Football Apparel Digital Product Director ~ Pro Football Content Marketing Specialist ~ Pro Football Digital Content Associate ~ Pro Football Digital Content Coordinator ~ Pro Football Digital Content Producer

~ Pro Football Digital Signage Technician ~ Pro Football Digital Content Specialist ~ Pro Football Digital Marketplace Director ~ Pro Football Digital Media Coordinator ~ Pro Football Digital Media Manager ~ Pro Football DTC Capabilities Director ~ Pro Football Ecommerce Content Specialist ~ Pro Football Media Production Specialist ~ Pro Football Social Media Coordinator ~ Pro Football Social Media Manager ~ Pro Football Social Media Motion Graphics Artist and Animator ~ Pro Football Temporary Digital Content Producer ~ Program Content Coordinator (Part-Time) ~ Program Coordinator ~ Program Integration Coordinator ~ Program Manager ~ Project Content Associate ~ Project Coordinator ~ Project-Designer II Motion Graphics ~ Project Lead/Project Architect ~ Project Manager ~ Project-Marketing Coordinator ~ Project Manager (Timing) ~ Project Writer ~ Recurring Production Assistant ~ Recurring-Remote Talent Statistician (Event) ~ Remote Operations Specialist ~ Remote Productions Senior Financial Analyst ~ Replay Operator ~ Replay Operator (Freelance) ~ Replay Operator Production Trainee ~ Researcher ~ Research Associate ~ Research Manager ~ Resource Coordinator (Personnel & Facility Scheduling) ~ Retail Accountant ~ Retail Coordinator ~ Retail Project Manager ~ Retail Sales Associate ~ Retail Sales Specialist ~ Retail Senior Graphic Designer ~ Robotic Camera Operator ~ Reporter and Football Beat Writer ~ Run Club Coordinator ~ Safety Engineer ~ Sales & Hospitality Director ~ Sales Associate ~ Sales Associate National Accounts ~ Sales Care Specialist ~ Sales (College Sports Recruiting) ~ Sales Facilitator ~ Sales Integration Manager ~ Sales Manager ~ Sales Operations Coordinator ~ Sales Operations Manager ~ Scheduling Coordinator ~ Seasonal Field Marketing Assistant ~ Senior Accountant ~ Senior Business Data Analyst ~ Senior Business Systems Analyst ~ Senior Content Systems Engineer ~ Senior Data Engineer ~ Senior Data Privacy Analyst ~ Senior Deputy Editor ~ Senior Director Digital Technology ~ Senior Director Sports Marketing ~ Senior Editor ~ Senior Experiential Marketing Manager ~ Senior Financial Analyst ~ Senior Graphic

Designer ~ Senior Interactive Designer ~ Senior Marketing Manager ~ Senior Media Relations Associate ~ Senior Producer ~ Senior Producer/Editor ~ Senior Product Manager (Snow Sports) ~ Senior Project Management Office Manager ~ Senior Project Manager ~ Senior Property Accountant ~ Senior Public Relations Manager ~ Senior Social Media Coordinator ~ Senior Software Engineer ~ Senior Staff Accountant ~ Senior Tax Analyst ~ Senior Technical Project Manager ~ Senior UI Designer ~ Senior Video Workflow Engineer ~ Service Desk Associate ~ Shared Accountant ~ Short Form Managing Editor ~ Show/Broadcast Producer ~ Site Manager ~ Soccer Sports Data Specialist ~ Social Content Strategist ~ Social Media & Content Manager ~ Social Media Associate ~ Social Media Coordinator ~ Social Media Graphics Producer ~ Social Media Manager ~ Social Media Marketing ~ Social Media Marketing Associate ~ Social Media Marketing Director ~ Social Media Platform Strategist ~ Social Media Preditor ~ Social Media Production Assistant ~ Social Media Senior Manager ~ Social Media Specialist ~ Social Video Producer/Editor ~ Software Engineer ~ Sponsorship Sales Director ~ Sport Category Financial Analyst ~ Sports Account Executive ~ Sports Anchor/Reporter ~ Sports and Entertainment Sales Coordinator ~ Sportsbook CRM Manager (Sportsbook Online Strategic Responsibilities) ~ Sportsbook Producer ~ Sportsbook Promotions Specialist ~ Sports Broadcasting ~ Sports Content Researcher ~ Sports Content Reviewer ~ Sports Designer ~ Sports Director ~ Sports Editor ~ Sports Instructor ~ Sports Marketing Director ~ Sports Media Sales Professional ~ Sports/Non-Sports Grader ~ Sports Page Editor ~ Sports Play By Play Board Operator ~ Sports Production Associate ~ Sports Program Associate ~ Senior Project Manager ~ Sports Reporter ~ Sports Reporter/Editor ~ Sports Research Junior Analyst ~ Sports Senior Editor ~ Sports Site Manager ~ Sports Writers ~ Staff Accountant ~ Strategic Insights Director ~ Storage Archive Engineer ~ Store Logistics Manager ~ Store Operations Manager ~ Student Sports Agent ~ Studio Coordinator ~ Summer Camp

Sports Area Director ~ Supply Chain Financial Analyst ~ Talent Manager ~ Talent Marketing Senior Manager ~ Talent Producer ~ Talent Senior Director ~ Team Brands Community Manager ~ Technical Director ~ Technical Lead ~ Technical Product Manager ~ Technical Project Manager ~ Technology Procurement Director ~ Temporary Digital Content Producer ~ Tennis Event Host ~ Ticker Operator ~ Ticket Operations Manager ~ Ticket Researcher ~ Trackman Operator ~ Traffic Coordinator ~ Training Center Coordinator ~ Training Specialist ~ Transmission Operator I ~ Transmission Operator II ~ Transmission Operator (Freelance) ~ Trending Writer ~ Tutor Coordinator ~ TV Account Manager ~ UFC Rendering Engineer ~ Unannounced Project Creative Lead ~ University Desk Copy Editor ~ Vendor Management Manager ~ Venues Community Support Manager ~ Video Ad Product Manager ~ Videographer and Editor ~ Video Editor ~ Video Manager ~ Video Operations Manager ~ Video Operator ~ Video Operator (Part-Time Staff) ~ Video Production Specialist ~ VizRt Operator ~ Warranty Repair Operator ~ Weekend Sports Anchor/Reporter ~ Women's Graphic Designer II ~ Youth Camp Site Technical Director ~ Youth Events Support.

STUDENT AND STUDENT-ATHLETE PLAN B BOOK
ALL STUDENTS, AND PARTICULARLY, STUDENT-ATHLETES, "DO YOU HAVE A PLAN B?

Professional Occupation Questionnaire for Student Academic & Career Developmental Exposure

Name: Andrew Stockey

Your Current Job Title and/or the Job You're Most Known for Participating: News Anchor/Sports Director WTAE-TV Pittsburgh
Number of Years in Current Position or Number of Years in the Position You're Most Known for Participating: 23
List the Previous Job Titles You've Had: Sports Director WALA-TV Mobile, Sports Reporter/Anchor WTIC-TV Hartford
List College Major(s), Master Degree(s), Doctoral Degree(s): B.S. Telecommunications, Ohio University Honors College

1. **Who inspired you the most?** My father was the one who inspired me the most.

2. **What motivated you during the pursuit of your career?** The desire to be the hardest worker at each stop motivated me in pursuing my career.

3. **Who or what influenced you to achieve your goal(s) as a professional?** I do not know if it was someone, as much as, it was the desire to succeed.

4. **What goal(s) did you set for yourself in attempting to reach your career aspiration(s)?**
   My goals were to help my company/television station to be the best, and in turn, my career grew alongside.

5. **What were your greatest strengths that you executed as a professional within your career?**
   The skills of leadership, communication and the ability to get answers on my own were my greatest strengths.

6. **What most challenged you during your journey to becoming the professional in your occupation?**
   The limitations of my field which, in essence, means the constrictions of time to fit in the television format challenged me.

7. **How did you manage your weaknesses within your occupation?**
   Hard work and a desire to succeed while learning how to succeed where I had failed before, is how I managed my weaknesses.

8. **How important was time management in performing well on your job?** Time management is essential because my field is always dictated by deadlines. It's critical to make sure that when it's time for you to present, you are ready.

9. **How much of your educational background factored into obtaining success in your field of work?** Again, my educational background was critical to my success. At Ohio University, I learned how to get answers and how to find solutions on my own. The skills I possess are ones that I still use today.

10. **What was your greatest accomplishment as a professional?** Being able to cover both political conventions as a news anchor in successive weeks during 2016, was my greatest accomplishment.

11. **Why did you or do you work?** Work gives me purpose and identity. I don't know if I can see a life without work.

12. **What did you or do you value most about your occupation?** I value learning all about the community I call home. My vocation gives me the privilege of appreciating the many different angles and views of the community.

STUDENT AND STUDENT-ATHLETE PLAN B BOOK
ALL STUDENTS, AND PARTICULARLY, STUDENT-ATHLETES, "DO YOU HAVE A PLAN B?

Professional Occupation Questionnaire for Student Academic & Career Developmental Exposure

Name: Joe Butler

Your Current Job Title and/or the Job You're Most Known for Participating: Director of Joe Butler's Metro Index Scouting Service

Number of Years in Current Position or Number of Years in the Position You're Most Known for Participating: 42 years

List the Previous Job Titles You've Had: Head Football Coach/Teacher at St. Bernard's Grade School – Mount Lebanon, PA

List College Major(s), Master Degree(s), Doctoral Degree(s): Bachelor of Science in Secondary Ed - California University of PA, Received teaching certificate from University of Pittsburgh Master's Degree Program (few credits short from a Master's Degree in Education, started scouting business and did not finish)

1. **Who inspired you the most?** My parents were very influential in my career development.

2. **What motivated you during the pursuit of your career?** I wanted to be a basketball/football scout.

3. **Who or what influenced you to achieve your goal(s) as a professional?** Self-motivation was what influenced me.

4. **What goal(s) did you set for yourself in attempting to reach your career aspiration(s)?** Working hard, treating everyone the same, eliminating jealousies, and possessing a positive outlook toward the business community and my peers are all goals I set for myself.

5. **What were your greatest strengths that you executed as a professional within your career?** As a professional, my greatest strengths were being organized, returning phone calls, concentrating on having good business relationships by not burning any bridges, having a willingness to help other people and committing myself to not being greedy.

6. **What most challenged you during your journey to becoming the professional in your occupation?** Focusing on being myself and being productive is how I evolved during my career. This caused me to overcome and succeed.

7. **How did you manage your weaknesses within your occupation?** I managed my weaknesses by evaluating my mistakes and correcting them.

8. **How important was time management in performing well on your job?** Preparation eases the pain of improperly planned time management.

9. **How much of your educational background factored into obtaining success in your field of work?** Getting a proper education creates discipline, and self-discipline creates positive results.

10. **What was your greatest accomplishment as a professional?** My greatest accomplishment was enjoying working with other people in my industry and witnessing the promotion of others, not myself.

11. **Why did you or do you work?** I am fortunate to have a job I like, and I will continue to work at my age until I am not productive anymore. I refuse to take another position for the mere fact that I do not want to take a young person's opportunity away. I endeavor to be an asset to the scouting service business to assist coaches in finding prospects.

12. **What did you or do you value most about your occupation?** I value assisting high school prospects by positioning them at the collegiate level while, at the same time, making the job for collegiate coaches easier.

Last Word of Encouragement: Keyword: Patience. Younger people entering the workforce need to be patient with their opportunities. It is human nature to rush into things, but taking time in an orderly fashion, and being patient will make your transition into the business field more rewarding. Young people need to take a conservative approach when deciding to spend personal money. Keep out of debt if you can. A person who is in continual debt will magnify stress. Having a series of college loan payments can make it rough for a college graduate entering the workforce, which in turn, can create an abundance of stress. Stress can create inconsistencies.

SPORTS TELEVISION JOBS

Account Executive ~ Account Services Executive ~ Ad Operations Coordinator ~ Ad Operations Senior Coordinator ~ Advertising and Program Standards Senior Editor ~ Art Director (Creative) ~ Assistant Chief Engineer ~ Assistant Editor ~ Associate Content Strategist ~ Associate Designer Motion Graphics ~ Associate Director ~ Associate Director I ~ Associate Editor (NFL) ~ Associate Director Mobile Enging (IOS Platform) ~ Associate Operator ~ Associate Producer ~ Associate Transmission Engineer ~ Audience Development Manager ~ Authentication Operations Coordinator ~ Baseball Business Development Coordinator ~ Brand Design Manager ~ Branded Content Associate Producer ~ Breaking News Associate Editor ~ Broadcast Associate ~ Broadcast Maintenance Engineer I ~ Broadcast Maintenance Engineer II ~ Broadcast Operations Manager (BOC) ~ Broadcast Production Workflows Manager ~ Business Analyst ~ Business Strategy and Operations Director ~ Camera Operator/Lead Studio ~ Character Model ~ Chief Communications and Development Officer ~ Client Service Coordinator ~ Client Service Representative ~ Client Strategy Senior Manager ~ College Conference Channels Producer ~ Communications Coordinator ~ Communications Manager ~ Community Coordinator ~ Community Manager ~ Computer Graphics Operator ~ Concept Design Art Director ~ Consumer Engagement Coordinator ~ Content Coordinator ~ Content Development Executive Director ~ Content Integration Director ~ Content Licensing Vice President ~ Content Miner ~ Content Product Manager ~ Content Programmer ~ Content Strategy and News Manager ~ Content Vice President ~ Coordinator Producer ~ Creative Assistant ~ Creative Director ~ Crewing Coordinator II ~ Customer Service Sports Senior Manager ~ Data Architecture Director ~ Database Administrator ~ Designer ~ Digital Account

Executive ~ Digital Content Distribution Associate Editor ~ Digital Content Specialist (NFL/MLB) ~ Digital Coordinator ~ Digital Creative Director ~ Digital Editor ~ Digital Editor Regional Networks ~ Digital Product Development Director ~ Digital Storytelling & Innovation Design Lead ~ Director of Business Operations ~ Direct-to-Consumer Content Strategy Director ~ Editor ~ Editorial Producer ~ Editor-In-Chief ~ Encodist ~ eSports Editor ~ eSports Writer ~ Experienced Premiere Multi-Cam Editor ~ Fantasy Content Associate Editor ~ Financial Reporting & Accounting Vice President ~ Freelance Digital Production Assistant ~ Freelance On-Air Graphics Operator ~ Freelance Production Assistant ~ Freelance Photographer ~ Freelance Robotic Camera Operator ~ Game Operations Associate ~ Games Event Management Manager ~ General Manager ~ Global Strategy Director ~ Golfer Care Specialist ~ Graphic Designer ~ Graphics Operator/Controller (Motion Graphics) ~ Highlight Producer ~ Human Resources and Payroll Coordinator ~ Human Resources Business Partner ~ Human Resources Director ~ Human Resources Manager ~ Human Resources/Payroll Manager ~ Infrastructure Operations Director ~ Ingest Operator I ~ Implementation Specialist ~ Integrated Media Associate Director ~ International Strategy Director ~ Internship Event Manager (Fairs & Convention) ~ Junior Graphics Designer ~ Junior Publicist ~ Lead Audio (A1) ~ Lead Content Strategist ~ Lead Designer Motion Graphics ~ Lead Studio/Camera Operator ~ Learning Development Manager ~ Logger/Subclipper ~ Managing Producer ~ Marketing Manager ~ Market Sales Manager ~ Media Operations Workflow Associate ~ Media Platform Associate Product Manager ~ Media Sales Representative ~ Metro Market Sales Manager (Account Management) ~ Mobile Developer ~ Motion Graphics Art Director ~ Motion Graphics Artist ~ Multimedia Journalist Sports ~ Multi-Platform Coordinator ~ Multi-Platform Editor ~ Multi-Platform Video Producer/Editor ~ NBA Insider ~ Network Analyst ~ Night Homepage Editor ~ Night-Side Graphics Designer ~ On-Air Graphics Operator ~ On-Air Graphics Senior Project Manager

~ On-Air Talent ~ Organizational Development Manager ~ Original Content & Brand Intelligence Senior Analyst ~ Original Live Studio Content Production Assistant ~ Pagination Desk Designer/Sports ~ Paralegal ~ Partner Care Services Specialist ~ Partner Services Temp ~ Partner Solutions Director ~ Partnership Development Director ~ Photo/Graphics Editor ~ Platform Client Solutions Associate Director ~ Plus Implementationist ~ Plus Specialist ~ Preditor ~ Premium Digital Lead ~ Producer ~ Product Development & Production Assistant Manager ~ Production Assistant ~ Production Coordinator ~ Product Manager ~ Program Director ~ Product Manager (Global Consumer Ad Product) ~ Program Integration Coordinator ~ Program Management Associate Director ~ Program Management Director ~ Project Coordinator ~ Project Manager ~ Recurring-Remote Graphics Interface Coordinator ~ Recurring-Remote Talent Statistician Event ~ Remote Crew Scheduler ~ Remote Traffic Coordinator II ~ Replay Operator ~ Researcher ~ Resource Coordinator (Personnel & Facility Scheduling) ~ Robotic Camera Operator ~ Run Coordinator ~ Sales Care Specialist ~ Scheduling Coordinator ~ Segment Producer I ~ Senior Content Systems Engineer ~ Senior Copywriter ~ Senior Deputy Editor ~ Senior Director Strategies & Creative Partnership ~ Senior Editor ~ Senior Financial Analyst ~ Senior Graphics Operator ~ Senior Interactive Designer ~ Senior Researcher ~ Senior Research Manager ~ Senior Social Producer (Predictive) ~ Senior Social Producer (Real Time) ~ Senior Software Engineer ~ Senior Software Engineer ~ Senior Technical Director ~ Senior Video Editor ~ Social Assistant Editor ~ Social Media and Communications Manager ~ Social Media Editor ~ Social Media Producer ~ Social Programmer Temp (NBA) ~ Software Engineer ~ Software Engineer II ~ Software Engineer III ~ Sponsorship Sales & Activation Account Services ~ Sponsorship Services Coordinator ~ Sports Account Executive ~ Sports Associate Producer ~ Sportsbook Producer ~ Sports Digital Streaming & Video Ops Producer ~ Sports Director ~ Sports Director (Live Event) ~ Sports Editor ~ Sports Media Sales

Professional ~ Sports News/Writer ~ Sports Producer (Live Event) ~ Sports Producer/Reporter ~ Sports Radio Producer/Board Operator ~ Sports Reporter ~ Sports Reporter Anchor ~ Sports Television Producing ~ Sports Transmission Engineer I ~ Sports Transmission Engineer II ~ Sports Writer ~ Staff Writer ~ Strategic Insights Director ~ Strategies & Creative Partnerships Coordinator ~ Studio Technical Direction Manager ~ Supervising Director ~ Talent Acquisition Vice-President ~ Talent Booking Senior Director ~ Talent Director ~ Technical Director ~ Technical Manager ~ Technical Operations Analyst I ~ Technical Operations Analyst II ~ Technology Manager ~ Technology Vice President ~ Television Marketing Manager ~ Television Researcher ~ Television Sports Network Researcher ~ Temporary Client Service Coordinator ~ Ticker Researcher ~ Traffic Coordinator ~ Transmission Operator ~ Transmission Specialist ~ Transmission Specialist II ~ Transmission Specialist III ~ Transmission Systems Technician I ~ UI Designer ~ Unity Technical Artist ~ Vice President Director ~ Vice President of Product Management ~ Videographer/Editor ~ Video Operations Assistant Manager ~ Video Operator.

STUDENT AND STUDENT-ATHLETE PLAN B BOOK
ALL STUDENTS, AND PARTICULARLY, STUDENT-ATHLETES, "DO YOU HAVE A PLAN B?

Professional Occupation Questionnaire for Student Academic & Career Developmental Exposure

Name: William Tormay "Bill" Doorley

Your Current Job Title and/or the Job You're Most Known for Participating:
For most of my career, my title was Writer/Producer, and I worked for a company here in Pittsburgh that made "industrial films," films and videos for corporations, government agencies, etc. I was also briefly a writer/producer for Cortina Productions in Washington, DC, just before the bottom dropped out of the economy. I'm still writing and producing, but on independent projects, taking temp jobs to pay the bills. It's part of having a career in the arts.

Number of Years in Current Position or Number of Years in the Position You're Most Known for Participating:
I was a writer/producer at The Magic Lantern in Pittsburgh for about 25 years.

List the Previous Job Titles You've Had:
Planetarium Operator and Lecturer, Dispatcher (for a trucking company), Museum Aide (Smithsonian), Technical Specialist (Apple Store), Bookmobile Driver/Clerk, and a retail cashier more times than I care to remember.

List College Major(s), Master Degree(s), Doctoral Degree(s):
Bachelor of Arts, 1982, Communications/Visual Media, American University, Washington, DC
Master of Arts, 2011, Communications/Producing for Film and TV, American University, Washington, DC

1. **Who inspired you the most?** I think my father was my greatest inspiration. He never forced me to choose a particular career, but he did insist that I work hard at whatever I chose to do. He was general manager of a trucking company when Pittsburgh was still the world's steel capital. He had to deal both with labor union bosses (once he came home with bullet holes in his car) and steel company executives. It's difficult to say which was more ruthless. Through it all, my father remained an honest man, true to himself and his principles. That is the standard I apply to my life, whether I'm directing a film crew or scanning coupons at Walgreen's.

2. **What motivated you during the pursuit of your career?** It's hard to say. My family, as well as the whole Pittsburgh region, has a strong work ethic. No matter what, you must support yourself and your family to the best of your ability. Beyond that, I was fortunate enough to have a job doing things I loved to do like writing, traveling, and making films. That made it easy to get out of bed and go to work in the morning.

3. **Who or what influenced you to achieve your goal(s) as a professional?** As I already mentioned, my father influenced me the most. It was my mother who "gave

permission" for me to be a writer and filmmaker, which weren't necessarily, considered "real jobs" in Pittsburgh. My teachers at American University were all working filmmakers, not academic aesthetes, and they were able to give me the tools I needed to build a career. Less directly, I've always enjoyed science and technology, and my thinking has been influenced by many writers of these subject matters. To be a good writer, you have to read works written by good writers.

4. **What goal(s) did you set for yourself in attempting to reach your career aspiration(s)?** Right now, I want to move into teaching film and writing at the university level. So, I'm looking for opportunities for classroom teaching, writing articles for publication, and making films to enter in festivals. But I've never had serious long-term goals, only relatively short-term goals like "graduate," "finish this project," or "get on the faculty." You might say my thinking is more tactical rather than strategic. On one hand, this allows me to be flexible and respond to setbacks (like the economic slump of 2008) or opportunities as they arise. On the other, though, it makes important things like building a network of professional colleagues more difficult. It also gives me an eclectic resumé that some employers find difficult to evaluate. They don't look for someone who did "a little bit of this and a little bit of that." That's made it harder for me to find a job during the inevitable dry spells in the film production.

5. **What were your greatest strengths that you executed as a professional within your career?** My greatest strength is my ability to write a coherent paragraph with correct punctuation and spelling. For that, I thank my high school English teacher, who had us memorize rules from *Elements of Style* by Strunk and White. Related to that is my ability to present ideas to others, whether it's a group of people at a conference or one-to-one as a volunteer computer assistant at the library. (That's why I think I'd be a good teacher.) I can say without false modesty that, if nothing else, I present myself well on paper and in person. All those clichés about dressing appropriately, good grooming, good posture, and so on are very true and incredibly important, and I learned all about it from my father.

6. **What most challenged you during your journey to becoming the professional in your occupation?** Frankly, the greatest danger with any kind of art career is not making enough money to survive. My challenge was recognizing when I had to separate my work as a writer and filmmaker from the need to pay the bills. Looking back, I realize now that I feared to take a desk job pushing paper for a corporation was somehow connected with failing as a writer and filmmaker. Today, I still consider writing and filmmaking my career even though I take temporary contract jobs to make ends meet. I think the lesson is the same for anyone. Whether you're an artist, not that I consider myself an "artist", or an engineer, it is all the same. There are always times when you do what you have to do rather than what you want to do or what you were

trained to do. I finally chose to treat those times as opportunities to learn new skills. For instance, I've never liked talking on the phone, but the telephone is the producer's most valuable tool. Working as a call center operator, I've overcome my feelings about phone calls, and that has helped me with my film career and my life in general.

7. **How did you manage your weaknesses within your occupation?** The short answer is "not very well," I'm afraid. One of my weaknesses is that I'm stubborn. If I'm not careful, I'll pursue something long past the point of diminishing returns. This manifested itself in an obstinate refusal to look for work outside the film and video production business. That would be okay in a job that combined the creative and the technical, like being videographer or editor. I know how to use a camera and lights, and I'm competent at the editing console, but my strengths are in writing and producing. In my industry, writers/producers are running the production companies. They don't hire writers/producers. (They used to, but not since the digital revolution changed everything.) Thus I wasted time and energy and put myself through a lot of stress just because I wouldn't let go of an idea.

8. **How important was time management in performing well on your job?** Time management has been a vital part of every job I've ever held. Let's be clear. There's a lot more to time management than keeping to a schedule or punching a clock. Time management is all about using your time well, and I'm not naturally good at it. I have to work hard every day

too, as Kipling wrote, "fill the unforgiving minute with sixty seconds worth of distance run." It's hard, and I don't always do well, but when I do, I finish the day with a great sense of satisfaction.

9. **How much of your educational background factored into obtaining success in your field of work?** I've had some great teachers, again, beginning with my father who loved history and geography and learning for the joy of learning. My formal education covered a lot of fields, from literature to science, but what it really gave me was the ability to learn, to organize ideas, and to present those ideas to others. When making a film for a corporate client, I could become an "instant expert" on their business because my education taught me how to learn, and I've kept right on learning long after my degrees were gathering dust in their frames.

10. **What was your greatest accomplishment as a professional?** My greatest accomplishment at "The Magic Lantern" was a half-hour film I wrote, produced, and directed for the National Science Foundation (NSF). We always worked as a team, and this film was no exception, but the project was mine from the very beginning. I wrote the proposal. I scouted the locations on college campuses all over the country, and I led the crews on the majority of the shooting trips. The NSF film combined everything I love, such as: writing, filmmaking, travel, and science and technology.

11. Why did you or do you work? We work to have a place to live, to put food on the table, and pay our bills. That's the practical aspect of work. I think society requires us to have a job, if not a career. It's part of our public identity. How often have you been asked, "What do you do?" Deeper still, I believe that being occupied and useful is part of our human nature. Our minds and bodies are geared toward activity, and work is a purposeful activity that can be very satisfying, even if it's working on an assembly line or at the drive-up window at a restaurant. Work also gives us the opportunity to meet people, and humans are social creatures that need personal contact with others to be physically and mentally healthy. I can't imagine myself retiring or living a life of leisure. I hope to continue to work right up to the end.

12. What did you or do you value most about your occupation? I think what I value most about my occupation is communication. Writers, filmmakers, and artists of all kinds--though, again, I consider myself more of a craftsman than an artist--are ultimately communicators. I not only value the mission of presenting information and ideas to others, but I value the process of gathering, learning, and organizing. This mission of communication has introduced me to many people (like the Lieutenant Governor of Pennsylvania), places (like the control room at Three Mile Island where the accident unfolded), and stories (like that of the Pittsburgh *Courier*, an African-American newspaper) I would never have known otherwise.

13. **What advice would you give your 8th-grade self as a student preparing for a future career?** My eighth-grade career plan was to become an engineer and then a NASA astronaut. (The Space Shuttle was then in development.) At the same time, I now realize my talent for writing was starting to manifest itself. I think I would have encouraged my younger self to pay more attention to it even while studying engineering. I would not have suggested that "he" abandon the dream of space flight, but I would have encouraged writing and communicating as a powerful tool for any career. Perhaps if I'd consciously started to develop my talent then, I might have discovered my career much earlier.

14. **Please feel free to list any future projects you are working on you'd like to promote to list in this Plan B Book:** I'm finishing a short film. The film profiles a remarkable woman who was a well-known neurologist at Walter Reed Army Medical Center. She pioneered the brain trauma treatments that were invaluable to our troops in Iraq and Afghanistan. At the height of her career, she contracted a degenerative nerve disease and became her own experiment in how to live a full life in spite of limitations and complications. I hope to finish it by the end of 2018.

Encouragement for our youth: I've tried to answer this question many times, and I keep coming up with new thoughts. To list them all would make me sound like a motivational speaker. If I had to pick one, though, I'd tell kids to always be open to new ideas and experiences. Fear can be a useful emotion. It keeps us out of danger. But unless we accept some risks, we can't grow and learn. You can train yourself to understand and accept risk by starting small. Maybe the best method is to introduce yourself to someone you want to meet or taking an offer to travel abroad. Then when the big risks come along, you'll be prepared, and you'll find your life is rich and interesting.

GLOSSARY

Abundance - a very large quantity of something
Achieve – **1)** to carry out successfully or **2)** to attain as the result of a person's effort
Acquire – **1)** to obtain an object or **2)** asset for oneself or **3)** to learn or develop a skill, habit or quality
Adage - a proverb or short statement expressing a general truth
Adroit - clever or skillful in using the hands or mind
Aesthete - a person who has or affects to have a special appreciation of art and beauty
Affluent – **1)** a group or area having a great deal of money or **2)** wealthy
Aforementioned - indicating a thing or person previously mentioned
Aptitude - a natural ability to do something
Aspire – **1)** desiring and working to achieve a particular goal or **2)** having aspirations to attain a specified profession, position, etc.
Astute - having or showing an ability to accurately assess situations or people and turn this to one's advantage
Autonomy – **1)** a person's freedom from external control or influence or **2)** independence
Career – **1)** a field for or pursuit of consecutive progressive achievement especially in public, professional, or business life or **2)** a profession for which one trains and which is undertaken as a permanent calling
Challenge - a call to take part in a contest or competition

Cliché - a phrase or opinion that is overused and betrays a lack of original thought or **2)** stereotype
Coherent – **1)** logical or **2)** consistent or **3)** united as or forming a whole
Competent - having the necessary ability, knowledge, or skill to do something successfully
Competitive - inclined, desiring, or suited to compete
Concierges - a hotel employee whose job is to assist guests by arranging tours, making theater and restaurant reservations, etc
Consciously - perceiving or noticing with controlled thought or observation
Degenerative - tending to decline and deterioration
Diagnosis - the art or act of identifying a disease from its signs and symptoms
Dictated – **1)** say or read aloud or **2)** have words typed, written down, or tape recorded
Diminish – to make (someone or something) seem less impressive or valuable
Discrimination - the unjust treatment of different categories of people or things, especially on the grounds of race, age, or sex
Disseminate - spread or disperse (something, especially information) widely
Diversified – **1)** to make or **2)** to vary or **3)** to enlarge or vary the range of products or the field of operation of (a company)
Eclectic - developing ideas, style, or taste from a broad and diverse range of sources
Endeavor - an attempt to achieve a goal
Enthusiast – a person who is highly interested in a particular activity or subject
Envision – **1)** imagine as a future possibility or **2)** visualize or **3)** to picture to oneself
Equity - the quality of being fair and impartial

Experiential – 1) involving or 2) based on experience and observation
Expertise – superior skill or knowledge in a particular field
Exploit - make full use of and to get a benefit from a resource
Fortitude – 1) courage in pain or 2) adversity
Genetic – 1) relating to the origin or arising from a common origin or 2) relating to heredity
Guarantee - assurance for the fulfillment of a condition
Illustrious - well known, respected, and admired for past achievements
Imperative – 1) an essential or urgent thing or 2) of vital importance
Impetus - the force that makes something happen or happens more quickly
Incurable - a person who cannot be cured of a disease or sickness
Inevitable - certain to happen; unavoidable
Integral – 1) necessary to make a whole complete or 2) essential or 3) fundamental
Integrity – 1) the quality of being honest and having strong moral principles or 2) moral uprightness
Intrinsically - in an essential or natural way
Introvert - a shy person
Job – a paid position of regular employment
Keener - a person who is extremely eager or enthusiastic
Legacy - something transmitted by or received from an ancestor or predecessor or from the past
Manifest – 1) display or show (a quality or feeling) by one's acts or appearance or 2) to demonstrate
Modesty - the state of being unassuming or moderate in the estimation of one's abilities
Nourish - to promote the growth of

Obstinate – stubbornly refusing to change or overcome despite attempts to persuade
Occupation - the principal business of one's life
Paradigm – **1)** a typical example or pattern of something or **2)** a model
Passion – **1)** a strong liking or desire for or **2)** devotion to some activity, object, or concept
Perennial – **1)** lasting or existing for a long time or **2)** enduring or **3)** continually recurring
Persevere - continue in a course of action even in the face of difficulty
Persistence - firm continuance in a course of action in spite of difficulty or opposition
Predicated – found or base something on
Prioritization – to rank something or something in the order of importance
Procrastination - the action of delaying or postponing something
Professional - a person engaged in a specific activity as one's main paid occupation rather than a pastime
Proficient – competent or skilled in doing or using something
Proponent - a person who supports a concept, a proposal, or a project
Psyche - the human soul, mind, or spirit
Purpose - **1)** something set up as an object or end to be attained or **2)** intention or **3)** to propose as an aim to oneself
Rapport - a close and harmonious relationship in which the people or groups concerned understand each other's feelings or ideas and communicate well
Relentlessly – to make an effort to accomplish something over and over again

Relevant – 1) closely connected or 2) appropriate to what is being done or considered or 3) appropriate to the current time, period, or circumstances

Remission - a relief or stoppage of the disease or sickness

Resilience – 1) the capacity to recover quickly from difficulties or 2) toughness

Scholar - a person who is highly educated or has an aptitude for study

Segregation - the enforced separation of different racial groups in a country, community, or establishment

Specialized - designed, trained, or fitted for one particular purpose or occupation

Stimulus - a thing that causes activity or energy in someone or something or 2) an incentive

Trends - a general direction in which something is developing or changing

Underprivileged – (of a person) not enjoying the same standard of living or rights as the majority of people in a society

Vocation – a strong desire for a certain career or course of action or 2) the work in which a person is regularly employed

REFERENCE PAGE

Dill, Kathryn. (2014, August 28). *The Sports-Related Jobs With The Strongest Growth.* Retrieved from https://www.forbes.com/sites/kathryndill/2014/08/28/the-sports-related-jobs-with-the-strongest-growth/#1749b4962955

Auerbach, Debra. (2014, August 28). *22 of the Fastest Growing Sports Jobs.* Retrieved from https://www.careerbuilder.com/advice/twenty-two-of-the-fastest-growing-sports-jobs

The Top 10 Sports Careers for Non-Athletes. (n.d.). Retrieved from https://thebestschools.org/careers/top-sports-careers-non-athletes/

Top 10 Cities with the Highest Sports-Related Job Growth. (n.d.). Retrieved from https://www.forbes.com/pictures/fjle45idgh/10-cities-with-the-highest-sports-related-job-growth/#6afc230d7f64

Myworkinsports. (2018, May). Retrieved from https://www.workinsports.com/usrhome.asp

Money Magazine and Sports Illustrated. (June 2018). Retrieved from http://time.com/money/4695629/best-colleges-sports-lovers/

Top 10 Colleges for Sports Lovers. (n.d.). Retrieved from http://time.com/money/4695629/best-colleges-sports-lovers/

Merriam-Webster.com (2018, May). Retrieved from https://www.merriam-webster.com

Google.com (2018, May), Retrieved from https://www.google.com

Gordon, V. N. (1995). *The undecided college student: An academic and career advising challenge* (2nd. ed.). Springfield, IL: Charles C. Thomas.

HOPING YOU WORK IN A JOB OF YOUR PASSION TO POSITIVELY IMPACT YOUR OCCUPATION AND OTHERS' LIVES TO HIGHER HEIGHTS!!!

It's better to give than receive, therefore, be the assist to bless someone else's life!!!

VISIT OUR WEBSITE AT:
www.vitaminfoodsinc.com

INDEX

A

Accountant: 13, 19, 28-32, 98-99, 157, 160-61
Accounting: 19, 47-48, 83, 94, 97-98, 126, 146, 170
Account Manager: 19, 29-31, 83, 125-26, 128, 130, 147, 154-55, 158, 162
Acquisition: 26, 32, 83-84, 100, 112, 125, 130, 154-55, 172
Administrative Assistant: 13, 25, 41-43, 94-95, 97-98
Administrator: 19, 25-26, 28-31, 45, 63, 66, 97-100, 156-57, 169
Advertising: 83, 154, 169
Advisor: 30, 82, 158
Analyst: 12, 19, 25-31, 41, 47-48, 66, 84, 93, 95, 97-98, 112, 125-30, 154-162, 169-172
Analytics: 26-27, 32, 47, 83, 94-95, 126, 128, 155-56, 158
Anchor: 130, 161-63, 165, 172
Animator: 100, 154, 160
Apparel: 30, 83, 94-95, 128, 154, 154
Aquatics: 25, 31, 93, 100
Art: 27, 30, 62, 65, 125, 155-56, 169-70, 182-83
Architect/ Architecture: 98, 126, 159-60, 169
Associate: 19, 23, 25-27, 29, 30-32, 40-44, 47-48, 58, 70, 83, 85-86, 93-94, 96, 100, 112, 125-26, 129-30, 143-48, 154-55,157-61. 169-71
Associate Producer: 25-26, 29, 154-55, 159, 169, 171
Athletic Director: 25, 31, 40-41, 43, 45, 58
Athletic Trainer: 15, 25, 28, 40-41, 47-50, 58, 83-84, 95, 97
Attorney: 25, 37
Auditor: 13, 29, 70

B

Baseball: 5, 40-41, 47, 83-85, 93-94, 102, 109, 132-34, 137, 140-42, 156, 159, 169
Basketball: 5, 7, 15, 36, 40-43, 46, 83, 87-88, 90, 93-94, 100-01, 121, 125, 137, 148, 166
Brand: 26, 30-32, 83-84, 95, 119, 125-27, 129-30, 146-47, 154, 157, 162, 169, 171

Broadcast: 26, 32, 83, 154, 161, 169
Broadcaster: 85, 100, 102, 130
Broadcasting: 25, 102, 104, 161
Budgeting Planning Coordinator: 26, 125, 154
Business: 7-9, 13, 23, 25-32, 37, 40-41, 47, 57, 66, 68, 83-91, 93, 95, 97-99, 115, 119, 121-22, 125-130, 137-39, 146, 154-55, 157-58, 160, 166-70, 177-78, 182, 188
Business Analyst: 26, 125, 127-30, 154-55, 157-58, 169
Business Development: 26, 83, 85, 93, 95, 121-22, 125, 154, 169

C

Camp: 26, 30, 32, 36, 48, 63, 86, 100-02, 114, 162
Chairman: 26, 33, 95
Cheerleader: 33, 41
Clerk: 14, 19, 173
Client: 26, 47, 83, 93, 95, 122, 129, 146, 154, 169, 171-72, 178
Coach: 14-15, 28, 32-33, 40-43, 45, 47-50, 59-63, 65-66, 73, 83, 93-95, 97-

189

104, 106-07, 109, 125, 131, 148, 151, 155, 158, 166, 168
College: 9, 17-18, 20, 23, 26, 33, 36-37, 41, 44, 46, 49, 51-52, 59-60, 66, 71, 77-82, 87, 90, 93, 95, 102-04, 107, 109, 121, 123, 125, 136-37, 139, 142-43, 148-49, 151-52, 155, 160, 163, 166, 168, 174, 178
Communication: 25-29, 47, 58, 83-84, 95-97, 121, 123, 125-28, 130, 155-56, 164, 169, 171, 174
Community: 26-27, 30-31, 34, 64, 83-84, 94-96, 101, 113-15, 117, 119-22, 125, 139, 155-56, 162, 165, 167, 169, 186
Consultant: 29-31, 47, 59, 61, 70, 93, 112, 127-28, 151, 158
Consumer Sales: 19, 125
Content: 26, 32, 48, 83, 85-86, 93-96, 99, 112, 125-26, 128, 130-31, 146, 154-62, 169-71
Contract: 26, 46, 176
Controller: 26, 47, 95, 170
Coordinator: 15, 19, 25-33, 40-43, 47-49, 70, 83-86, 93-101, 112, 116, 120, 125-31, 146-47, 154-62, 169-72
Copywriter: 26, 125, 128-30, 155, 171
Corporate Sales: 19, 26, 83, 125

Counselor: 31, 102, 136
Cross-Country: 40, 42
Customer: 26, 47, 56, 89, 122, 129, 169

D

Deputy: 26, 41, 100, 160, 171
Design: 27-28, 30, 32, 83-85, 96, 115, 125-130, 155-70
Designer: 28, 30-31, 96, 100, 125-27, 129-31, 154-58, 160-62, 169-72
Developer: 25, 93, 95, 97, 127-30, 170
Development: 20, 23, 25-31, 33, 37, 40-44, 47, 49, 52, 59, 66, 71, 77, 83-87, 93, 95, 99, 101-02, 109, 113, 120-22, 125, 127-29, 132, 136-37, 143, 146, 148, 151, 154-55, 158-59, 163, 166, 169-71, 173, 180
Digital: 25-30, 47, 83, 85, 93-96, 99, 125-27, 129-31, 146, 154-57, 159-60, 162, 169-71, 177
Digital Producer: 25, 154, 157
Director: 13, 15, 19, 25-33, 40-45, 47-48, 58-59, 70, 83, 85-86, 93-96, 98-101, 109, 112, 120, 125-30, 136, 146, 154-63, 166, 169-72
Distribution: 30, 47, 127-28, 155-57, 169

E

Ecommerce: 27, 83, 94, 96, 126, 130, 146, 156, 159-60
Editor(ial): 25, 27-32, 58, 70, 84-85, 93-94, 99-100, 112, 125-26, 128, 130-31, 146-47, 154-60
Education(al): 7-8, 21, 24, 33-35, 39, 50-52, 56, 59-60, 63-64, 68, 75, 77-82, 89-90, 107, 111, 123, 137, 140-42, 145, 148-49, 152-53, 164, 166, 168, 178
Engagement: 26, 48, 98, 138, 169
Engineer: 18, 27, 31-32, 68, 84, 98-99, 101, 126, 128-31, 143-45, 155-56, 158-62, 169, 171-72, 176, 180
Entertainment: 27, 29, 97, 116, 120, 122, 125-26, 128, 130, 161
Event(s): 12, 15, 25, 28-29, 31, 40-41, 67, 69, 84-85, 93, 95-99, 101, 108, 115, 126-27, 146, 156-58, 160, 162, 170-72
Executive: 13, 19, 25-28, 30-32, 40-44, 86, 97-98, 100, 112, 125, 127-30, 136, 146, 154, 156, 161, 169, 171, 174

F

Fantasy: 28, 30, 126, 156, 170

Finance: 24, 27-30, 32, 47, 66, 84, 86, 99, 101, 112, 115, 126-27, 156
Financial(ly): 18, 25-30, 39, 47, 53, 55, 57, 60, 66, 74, 79, 95-97, 141, 155-58, 160-62, 170-71
Fitness: 9, 15, 28, 30, 40, 42, 47, 49, 70, 84-85, 127, 157
Food(s): 11, 18, 28, 58, 70, 87, 91, 146, 157, 179
Football: 5, 15, 28, 40-43, 47-48, 58, 67, 70, 73, 83-85, 93-100, 103-07, 112, 121, 127, 129, 159-60, 166
Footwear: 28, 84, 100, 125-28, 130
Foundation: 5, 27-28, 41, 84, 90, 96-97, 113-17, 119, 133-34, 136-42, 178
Franchise Business Coach: 28, 47
Freelance: 27-28, 58, 157, 160, 162, 170
Fundraising: 28, 83, 115, 120, 157

G

Game Designer: 28, 30, 127
General Manager: 20, 25, 28, 42-43, 47, 97, 125, 127-28, 146-47, 170, 174
Global Benefits: 28, 127, 157
Golf(er): 5, 28, 40, 42-43, 47, 58, 93-94, 100, 126-27, 156-57, 170

Graduate Assistant: 10, 41-42, 58
Graphic Design: 27-28, 83-85, 127, 154-58, 160-62, 170
Group Sales: 19, 28, 31-32, 42, 84, 97, 100, 112, 127, 146, 157
Gymnastic(s): 50, 94, 151

H

Health: 2-4, 10-11, 18, 28, 30, 40, 42-43, 47, 49, 59, 62, 70, 73, 75-76, 78-81, 84, 87, 90, 102, 105, 113, 119, 124, 134, 148, 153, 157, 179
Hockey: 5, 50, 43, 93-94, 101, 121, 127, 156
Hospitality: 28, 42, 84-85, 160
Human Resources: 19, 23-24, 29, 31, 47, 84, 97, 100, 127, 146, 155, 157, 159, 170

I

Infrastructure: 26, 170
Instructor: 29-30, 42-43, 47, 93-94, 100-01, 128, 130, 161
IT (Information Technology): 29, 41, 84-86, 97, 125, 128, 154, 157

J

Journalist: 15, 130, 158, 170

K

Kinesiology: 40-42, 49

L

Lacrosse: 5, 40, 43, 58, 94, 100-01
Lead: 25, 28-31, 70, 94, 97, 112, 125-30, 146, 155, 157-60, 162, 169-71
League(s): 5, 26, 29, 36, 83, 93, 102, 109, 111, 121, 132-34, 141-42, 146, 158
Lecturer: 40-42, 49, 173
Licensing: 26, 130, 169
Logistics: 28-30, 32, 85-86, 97, 127-28, 130, 161

M

Manager: 13-14, 19-20, 25-32, 40-43, 47-48, 70, 83-85, 87, 93-101, 112, 116, 120, 125-31, 143, 146-47, 154-62, 169-72
Manufacturing: 29, 70, 87, 128, 158
Marketing: 12, 19, 25-30, 32, 37, 40, 42, 47-48, 58, 66, 83-86, 93-97, 99,

109, 112, 125-31, 146-47, 154-62, 170, 172
Martial Arts: 94
Media: 10, 26-27, 29-31, 40-42, 46-48, 58, 69, 83-86, 94, 96-98, 101, 112, 126-30, 142, 154-61, 170-71, 174
Membership: 30, 42, 47, 128, 158
Merchandise: 30, 56, 84, 93-98, 125, 127-28, 130, 158
MLB (Major League Baseball): 158, 170
Multimedia: 26, 30, 58, 84, 130, 155, 158, 170
Multi-Platform: 30, 94, 158, 170

N

NBA (National Basketball League): 20-21, 94, 100, 148, 150-51, 170-71
NFL (National Football League): 93, 102-05, 107, 154, 169-70
NHL (National Hockey League): 30, 94
Nutrition: 10, 28, 58, 70, 90, 146, 157-58

Office: 14, 26, 28, 30, 41, 83-84, 86-87, 99, 115, 146, 161
Olympic(s): 40-41, 59, 151, 153, 158

Outreach: 26, 83, 85, 97
Owner: 37, 39, 87, 94, 128, 150, 157

P

Partnership: 26, 29-31, 46, 84-85, 93-96, 98-99, 127-28, 138, 146, 155, 157-59, 171-72
Payroll: 19, 23, 32, 48, 98-100, 170
Physical Therapy(ist): 41, 43, 77-80, 82
Physician: 2, 70, 97-98, 114, 117
Pilates: 30, 47, 159
Plan: 3, 6, 8, 68, 90, 106, 137, 140, 180
Planned: 34, 115, 167
Planner: 12, 15, 29, 93, 126-27, 129-30, 158-59
Planning: 18, 248, 54, 84, 86, 96, 98-99, 115, 125-30, 140, 154-56, 158-59
Preditor (Editor & Producer): 112, 154, 159, 161, 171
President: 97-98, 100, 153
Producer: 13, 25-32, 41, 93-94, 96-100, 112, 125-28, 130-32, 147, 154-62, 169-73, 177
Production: 25, 27-28, 30, 32, 40, 42, 58, 83-86, 96-97, 99-100, 112, 126, 129-30, 140, 146-47, 154, 156-57, 159-62, 169-71, 173, 175, 177
Professor: 40-43, 49, 51, 59, 66-67, 71, 123, 137, 151-52

Program Coordinator: 25, 42, 70, 154, 158, 160
Program Director: 25, 30, 32, 43, 70, 93, 100, 126, 171
Project: 19, 22, 27, 30-32, 36, 39, 60, 67-69, 76, 85, 92, 98-99, 108, 120, 124-26, 129, 141-45, 154-57, 160-62, 170-71, 173, 175, 178, 180, 185
Project Manager: 27, 30-32, 98, 125-26, 129, 143, 154-57, 160-62, 170-71
Property: 26, 28, 31, 161
Psychology: 15, 43, 60-62, 70, 151-53
Publicist: 93, 170
Public Relations: 14, 25, 28, 30, 83-85, 98, 161

R

Recreation: 14-15, 40, 148, 153
Recruiting: 27, 42-43, 121, 125, 129, 160
Reporter: 99-100, 125, 127, 130, 155
Representative: 26, 28-32, 43, 47-48, 97, 99-100, 104, 112, 125, 127, 129-30, 146-47, 154, 159, 169-70
Research(er): 8, 12, 30, 63, 74, 84, 86, 89-90, 94, 113, 119, 124, 128, 139, 154, 156, 158-62, 171-72

S

Sales Manager: 25, 28-32, 83. 94, 97-100, 125, 129-30, 146-47, 156-58, 160, 170
Security: 14, 28, 93, -99, 129, 147, 156
Scout: 14, 26, 42, 83, 85, 93-95, 98, 98, 148, 150, 166, 168, 178
Soccer: 40-43, 58, 83, 85, 93-94, 100-01, 161
Social Media: 10, 30-31, 47-48, 83, 85-86, 94, 98, 112, 130, 142, 155, 157, 160-61, 171
Softball: 40, 43, 58, 84, 94, 100
Software: 28, 31, 85, 127-28, 130, 161, 171
Specialist: 6, 11-12, 14, 26-32, 42, 47-48, 66, 70, 85, 93-100, 112, 116, 125-31, 146-47, 154, 156-62, 170-73
Sponsorships: 26, 28, 31, 47, 85, 100, 115, 130, 161, 171
Sports Agent: 48, 100, 162
Sports Franchise: 28, 93
Sports Information: 58, 85
Sports Management: 10, 26, 29, 31, 86, 130
Sports Operations: 28, 126
Strategy: 26-30, 83-86, 93, 112, 126-28, 146, 155, 157-59, 169-70
Studio: 30, 32, 48, 112, 125-26, 130, 154, 158-59, 162, 169-72
Success(ful): 6-7, 15, 21, 24, 26, 35, 39, 45-46, 51, 53-56, 61-65, 68, 73-75, 81, 88-93, 107, 111, 122-23, 132, 134, 137, 140, 143, 145, 149, 152, 164-65, 168, 178
Supervisor: 19, 29, 47, 80, 95, 98-100, 129-30, 159
Swim/Swimming: 5, 58, 94, 100-01
System: 3, 12, 26, 28, 30-31, 34, 47, 69, 77, 95, 99, 129, 146, 160, 171-72

T

Technical: 31-32, 126, 128, 130, 154-55, 158, 161-62, 171-73, 177
Technology: 27, 29-30, 41, 80, 84, 89, 99-100, 157, 160, 162, 172, 175, 178
Tennis: 5, 41-43, 58, 84, 86, 93, 100, 162
Ticket Sales: 19, 28, 32, 41, 43, 48, 86, 97, 99, 130, 146-47, 156
Track and Field: 40-43, 59, 100, 130
Trackman: 32, 112, 162
Trainee: 19, 32, 155, 162
Trainer: 15, 25, 28, 40-41, 43, 47-50, 58, 83-84, 95, 97
Triathlon: 58, 100
Truck Driver: 32, 52-53, 55-56

V

Vice-President: 20, 26, 93-94, 97-101, 112, 125-27, 129-30, 146-47, 155, 157, 169-70, 172
Videographer: 32, 66, 69, 162, 172, 177
Video Production: 25, 27, 32, 58, 83, 86, 99, 162, 177
Volleyball: 5, 40, 43, 58, 69, 93-94, 101, 125, 131

W

Website: 10, 27-28, 32, 86, 97, 101, 115, 131, 147, 156, 159
Wellness: 10, 18, 32, 43, 49, 70, 75-76, 87, 90, 93
Writer: 83-84, 100, 162, 170-72, 174, 176

Y

Youth: 18, 26, 32, 53, 60, 74, 76, 86, 92-93, 97, 99, 101, 108, 121, 139, 142, 150, 162, 181

www.ingramcontent.com/pod-product-compliance
Lightning Source LLC
Chambersburg PA
CBHW071357290426
44108CB00014B/1590